BASKETBALL TIP-INS

BASKETBALL TIP-INS

100 Tips and Drills for Young Basketball Players

Nick Sortal

CONTEMPORARY BOOKS

Library of Congress Cataloging-in-Publication Data

Sortal, Nick.
    Basketball tip-ins : 100 tips and drills for young basketball players / Nick Sortal.
      p. cm.
    ISBN 0-8092-9953-4
    1. Basketball—Training.   I. Title.

  GV885.35 .S67   2000
  796.323—dc21   00-26738

Cover design by Nick Panos
Cover photograph copyright © Yellow Dog Productions/The Image Bank
Interior design by ABZORB Design, Inc.
Photo on page 205 copyright © Michelle Davis. Photos on pages 3, 11, 15, 17, 19, 25, 27, 29, 31, 33, 35, 43, 45, 47, 49, 53, 57, 61, 67, 73, 75, 81, 87, 89, 91, 93, 101, 103, 105, 107, 111, 113, 123, 125, 127, 129, 135, 137, 139, 141, 143, 145, 147, 150–151, 155, 157, 159, 161, 163, 165, 173, 175, 179, 181, 183, 199, 209, 211, 213, 217, 219, 221 are copyright © Mark Thomas. Photos on pages 5, 7, 13, 21, 23, 37, 41, 51, 55, 59, 63, 69, 71, 77, 79, 83, 85, 97, 99, 109, 117, 119, 121, 131, 149, 167, 171, 177, 185, 187, 189, 191, 195, 197, 201, 203, 215 are courtesy of the Sun-Sentinel.

Published by Contemporary Books
A division of NTC/Contemporary Publishing Group, Inc.
4255 West Touhy Avenue, Lincolnwood (Chicago), Illinois 60712-1975 U.S.A.
Printed in the United States of America
International Standard Book Number: 0-8092-9953-4
01 02 03 04 05 06 HP 19 18 17 16 15 14 13 12 11 10 9 8 7 6 5 4 3 2 1

CONTENTS

Chapter 3 **Passing**

Chapter 4 **Shooting**

Chapter 5 **Rebounding**

Chapter 6 **Defense**

Chapter 7 **Footwork**

Chapter 8 **The Big Man's Game**

Chapter 9 **Sidelines**

Chapter 10 **Coaching**

Chapter 11 **Your Body**

FOREWORD

In my career of coaching and playing basketball I have seen many changes in the game in terms of excitement, athleticism, and potential talent. The one tremendous negative has been the movement away from teaching and understanding the fundamental skills of the game. The most discouraging comment I can hear about a coach or player is that he or she "doesn't understand the game."

Having spent much of my life in the basketball-crazed states of North Carolina and Kentucky, I found two common denominators: kids start to play basketball at a very young age, and coaches spend considerable time drilling the fundamentals of the game. I consider Nick Sortal a "guardian of the game" because he has identified the need for skill development in the young players of south Florida. My challenge to those of you reading this skills book is to take these concepts and perfect them in your practices each day. Coaches, don't neglect teaching the basics; and players, don't neglect understanding the basics of the game.

When I coached at the University of Miami (Florida), our commitment to continually improve our players' fundamentals helped make ours a program on the rise. Take the challenge—become that player or coach people in the stands talk about when they say, "He understands the game." Best of luck in the pursuit of your basketball dreams.

J. Leonard Hamilton
Head Basketball Coach
Washington Wizards

ACKNOWLEDGMENTS

Basketball is a team game, so it's no accident that putting a book together about it is a group effort.

Even before we were dating, my wife, Robyn, would bring her videocamera to basketball games that I coached. That in itself was grounds for courtship, but watching the tapes with me afterward put her at the top of my list. (Her film on one opponent got us six points on out-of-bounds plays, and a victory, when my team got its rematch.) So it's not surprising that her well-placed "you-can-do-its"—as well as her journalistic advice—kept this book rolling along during dry spells.

Our driveway shooting games with Diane, Michelle, and Aaron provided enthusiasm for basketball, as well as some reminders about which fundamentals need to be conveyed.

Special thanks go to Cardinal Gibbons varsity coach Mark Wilson, who took in a coach without much experience (i.e., me) and was generous in sharing his knowledge of the game. And to all the Gibbons assistants along the way who have passed on a tip or two: Dick Littlefield, Charlie Stephenson, Glenn Pacek, Tom Spencer, and Bob Featherston.

Good coaches aren't afraid to share their material, and this book is better for the collective basketball mind of south Florida, from the volunteer dad at the youngest recreation league to those heading big-time programs at the high-school level and above. So many of you passed on a tidbit or two that will now be read by young basketball players—that's coaching at its purest level.

Sun-Sentinel manager John Christie suggested the idea of this book to NTC/Contemporary, a corporate cousin in the Tribune Company family. His vision, along with input from the Sun-Sentinel day news desk, conveys a spirit that every sports team should emulate.

All parents are special, but when you've been lucky enough to be born into a basketball environment you have to consider yourself especially blessed. So thanks to my father, Mike, and my mother, Violet, for teaching me about life, dreams, and the orange bouncing ball. And thanks for encouraging me to pursue them in the way I best saw fit.

INTRODUCTION: COACH YOURSELF

Basketball's beauty: a team game you can enjoy with skills you can learn on your own.

After watching everything from third-grade girls to NBA veterans (and every level in between) play basketball, there's one play I have never seen. A basketball coach has never put the ball into the basket for his team.

Former football coach Bill Parcells puts it another way, remembering back to his days as a high-school basketball player: "My coach told me that he can draw up a play to get me the ball five feet from the basket, but I'm the one who has to put it in."

The point is this: basketball, more than any other team game, can be self-taught. No one has to pitch a ball to you. No running back has to carry the ball toward you for you to work on tackling. Yes, Michael Jordan was blessed with talent and great coaches, but the person most responsible for his success was . . . himself.

More and more people are playing basketball; in 1998 10 million Americans played basketball once a week or more, and 42.4 million said they played sometime during the year. That's more than twice as many people as the next team sport, volleyball.

Girls' basketball continues to grow, with an increase in participation of almost 20 percent since 1990. (Note to all females: I used the pronouns *he* and *him* throughout this book not as a means of bias, but to avoid the awkward *him or her* construction that would otherwise muddy each page. The same goes for using *right-handed* instead of *right* and *left*.)

I wrote this book for the players—and parents of players—who want to learn more about basketball. When you read a tip that applies to your game, go out to your driveway hoop and walk through it.

Coach yourself. It's your game, and the more skills you have the better player you'll be.

Don't worry if you're the shortest or the skinniest. The biggest part of basketball is thinking: knowing when to shoot or when to pass . . . knowing to tell your teammate he has help to his right and to force his opponent that way . . . or knowing how to throw a bounce pass underneath those looooong arms the tall defenders are waving.

Bulging biceps and curvy calves make basketball easier, sure—but they're not the prime requirement. No, in basketball the number-one body part is safely hidden where no one can see it: it's the brain.

GETTING STARTED

1 TRIPLE THREAT

Your game depends on getting into this basic stance.

To be a good passer, shooter, or dribbler you must get your body in the proper position. Fortunately, the proper position for all three is the same, appropriately called the *triple threat position.* It should be a habit to get into triple threat each time you receive the ball.

The head is up and centered over your body. Your eyes are looking at the basket, but you can see the entire floor. Your feet are shoulder-width apart, with your weight evenly distributed and your knees bent. Your strong foot is slightly ahead of your weak one. Hold the ball near your dominant shoulder. (Let's assume players are right-handed.)

If you don't have the ball, be ready to get into triple threat as soon as the ball is passed to you. If you have your hands above your waist and your knees are bent, that's a good start.

When the ball is passed to you, your first move is to turn and face the basket. (A lot of coaches will yell "Turn and face!" to their players on every pass early in the season. If the habit is developed early, it becomes natural and players can go on to practice more advanced parts of the game.)

The biggest advantage of triple threat is its effect on the defense. Your defender doesn't know whether you're going to shoot, pass, or dribble—which means he can't guard your shot too close because you might drive. And he can't defend the drive too much for fear of the shot. And the defender's teammates can't come over and double-team you, because if they leave their opponents open you can pass the ball to your open teammate.

Of course, the triple threat is much more essential when you are near your own basket. There's no need to go into triple threat at half-court, because the defense knows you're not going to shoot. When you're obviously out of shooting range, it's sometimes better to hold the ball above your right knee. The knee braces the ball against your leg, and if a defender slaps down on it, he'll be beating the ball against your leg instead of tipping it away from you.

The triple threat: the all-purpose basketball position.

2 PIVOTING

Learn these four ways to spin.

Think of it almost like a Twister game:

- Left foot, back pivot

- Left foot, front pivot

- Right foot, back pivot

- Right foot, front pivot

By the time a basketball player is old enough to know the rules, he should know the four basic pivots. Proper footwork takes some time to integrate into your game, so it helps to learn early.

Learning to pivot isn't glamorous. Nobody ever says, "He's a great pivoter." It's just one of those things good players do that go unnoticed. But learning proper footwork with the basketball makes life easier. At the very least, it prevents traveling.

If you're not dribbling, you have to have at least one foot stationary. (I like to tell children to pretend that foot is nailed to the ground and they need to stomp on some bugs with the other foot.) You can spin as much as you want with that foot on the ground, but pick it up and it's traveling.

Whether you're on offense or defense, you pivot two ways: A front pivot is when your chest moves around the pivot foot. This is a good way to get in line with the basket for a shot. A rear, or back, pivot is when you lead with your rear end.

Learning to pivot well gets you out of trouble. To escape a defender, it's best to pivot away, sealing him off from the ball. Here are some pivoting tips:

- Be ready for action. Once you pivot, you'll have a new field of vision. Keep your hands and head up and ready.

- Keep your knees bent in a strong stance. Lift your heel to make a turn. The weight of your arms and elbows helps you keep your balance.

• Keep your feet at least shoulder-width apart. A lot of times, you'll be pivoting because of some contact. Don't get frustrated because of a little bump. Stay strong.

• If you're often called for traveling in games, cut down to two pivots. Right-handed players find it more natural to use left-foot pivots—especially out of triple threat position—and lefties can get by with only right-foot pivots.

Pivoting is a repetition skill. It needs to be done often at an early age to be useful. The best way to drill it into your game is to get in an offensive stance with the ball and have someone randomly call out the four types of pivots for you to execute.

To avoid trouble, use a back pivot. Turn your rear end and step backward.

3 FAKES

Don't be predictable.
Use your eyes and body to trick a defender.

Deception is a great equalizer. It can make a short player taller or make a slow one faster. But you must practice being tricky.

It's true in other sports, too. The wide receiver who runs only fly patterns becomes too predictable, and too easy to defend; the pitcher who throws only fastballs eventually gets rocked.

Put yourself in the position of the wide receiver. Your job is to get your defender to lean, even if it's just a little bit. That weight shift or loss of balance is just enough of an opportunity for you to get around him.

Watch any college basketball game on television. The ballhandlers fake passes into the middle of the lane to get more room for three-point shooters. When the defense starts to predict the single fake, the guards double-fake.

Here are my favorite fakes:

• **The shot fake:** For the first quarter of a game, watch who the shot-blockers are. When they come to guard you, raise the ball above your shoulders and eye the basket. The defenders don't have to leap to be vulnerable; once they raise their shoulders and come out of their stance you can drive around them.

But you must practice not faking yourself out. If you lose your balance while faking, you won't have enough leg drive to blow past the defender. So no foot fakes when you shot-fake, and keep your knees bent and your shoulders down.

- **The ball (or pass) fake:** The more tired a defender becomes, the more he will react to a ball fake. A good ball fake will buy more time for outside shooters, especially against a zone. From the top of the key you can fake an overhead pass to a teammate under the basket. The defense will react to help out. If you then pass to an outside shooter, the defender has to shift his momentum before running at the shooter. Try it: your team's shooters will love you for it.

- **Without-the-ball fakes:** These are among the most underpracticed moves by young players. If you want to cut to your right for the ball, you need to first get the defender leaning left. Make him think you're going in the opposite direction that you truly want to go.

Practice faking and cutting to the basket while having someone throw passes to you for layups. This is a more realistic way to practice scoring inside, as opposed to trotting in for short shots.

For all fakes: the defense will buy into your fake more if you use your eyes. Look first at where you want the defense to look. Only after they have taken the bait should you look at where you really want to go.

Practice your fakes at full speed. They must be believable to be successful.

Use a shot fake to get your defender in the air, then drive around him.

BALLHANDLING

4 THE WAY THE BALL BOUNCES

Dribble only when necessary; then do it well.

The first word about dribbling: *don't.*

Overdribbling is epidemic in basketball, especially at the younger levels. Look at any pickup game; a player will dribble until he is no longer guarded, and only then will he pass the ball.

More often than not, he should have passed the ball as soon as a teammate became open. After awhile, teammates stop trying to get open because they know they won't get the ball.

There are two times when dribbling is necessary:

1. To get out of trouble

2. To get the ball in better position for a basket

In traffic, keep your dribbling low and use your body to keep the defense away.

You're never too young to learn dribbling with each hand. Most right-handers can adequately go to the right well, but they become human turnovers once they go left. Start developing your left hand now.

Dribbling dos and don'ts:

• Dribbling is all fingertips. The palm should never touch the ball. Check your hand at the end of practice. If the palm is clean and the fingers are dirty, you're dribbling correctly.

• Keep your hand in the center of the ball for best control. Learn to dribble by feel so you can keep your head up to spot defenders and open teammates. Keep your hands below your waist.

• Learn to push the ball down hard by practicing typewriter dribbles. Those are six-inch dribbles, fast and hard. Do 25, then 50, then 100. This also builds up hand strength.

• When pressured by your defender, don't waste your dribble. Instead, pivot away from the defense, then use your dribble to get out of trouble.

To discourage dribbling, play halfcourt three-on-three games with no dribbling (a dribble becomes a turnover). It's a little chaotic at first, but eventually the players learn to pass and cut, and to set screens away from the ball. This develops the *pass first* attitude that's so important for a winning season.

The typewriter dribble builds up hand strength needed for strong dribbling.

5 GET IT BACK QUICK

Dribble hard and keep your hand low to avoid giving defenders time to steal.

Get it back quick.

If a basketball player dribbles the ball weakly, or starts a dribble from above his waist, he's in trouble. Quick defenders have a lot of time from the moment a dribbler pushes the ball to the floor until it returns to his fingertips again.

To shorten the time span, push the ball hard to the floor and keep your hand low. Hard dribbles minimize the time that you have no control over the ball. And if a teammate suddenly breaks open, you can get the ball to him more quickly.

To stay low while dribbling, bend your knees, not your back. A straight back helps you keep your head up so you can pass. Bent knees make for better balance and improve your ability to change direction.

A good way to practice dribbling the ball hard is called the *punching bag.* Alternate dribbling right and left hands on six-inch dribbles for about 50 dribbles. You'll feel almost like a bongo player, and the sound will be like a boxer hitting rapid-fire jabs at a punching bag. This exercise develops hand strength and helps you see how quickly the ball can actually bounce up to you.

Some of the worst habits develop at the playground while warming up. Wanting to impress friends, players will bounce the ball behind their back, carry it in front of them, then push it through their legs. And that's before the game starts.

The problem is that those habits become cemented into a player's game. Moves that look sensational warming up look weak when a defender plucks away another useless behind-the-back dribble—used trying to split a double-team, no less.

Many coaches employ the following rule: if you lose the ball while trying to dribble fundamentally, you'll get yelled at, but won't be replaced; lose the ball being a hotdog, and you're yanked out of the game.

Push the ball hard and keep your hand low.

6 THE SWEEP

To reach the promised land, come up with a countermove.

Part of dribbling is getting your body in the proper position to make a move. By nature, you'll want to set yourself up to dribble with your strong hand. But because the defense knows that, too, you need a countermove. Here is where the sweep comes in.

Imagine that you are in triple threat position on the wing and you want to drive to the basket. The defender properly has his left foot forward, taking away your right-hand dribble. If you want to get to the promised land, it'll have to be with your left hand. The key is quickly transferring your weight and intention—and, most important, the ball—from your right side to the left. Quickly *sweep* the ball across your belly and move your right foot outside of the defender's right foot, sealing him off. Then it's a hard left-hand dribble or two, and you're on your way.

Practice your sweep in slow motion against a passive defender. As you become more proficient, throw in a head fake to the right to throw the defender off-balance and get yourself some more room.

Also, make sure you don't hold the ball too far away from your body when changing from right to left. If you do, it will likely be poked away by your defender. In more competitive basketball, you may have to sweep the ball just above the floor, where defending it is a much more unnatural body motion.

After you've beaten your opponent with a sweep, don't give back the advantage you earned. Dribble on a straight line toward the basket, cutting off the defender you've just driven around. If you give him too much room, he'll simply cut you off again and you'll have more hard work to do.

Instead, be the one to initiate the contact. A lot of times the defense will be surprised and back off, afraid to foul. This is a part of your game that gets better if you practice it in pickup games, where a little bumping goes uncalled. Getting used to all kinds of contact will help you develop a toughness that will make it seem easy when you're playing a game with whistles.

If the defense has you stymied in one direction, quickly sweep the ball across your body and go the other way.

7 LEFT-HAND DRIBBLE

Strengthen your weak side to be a doubly effective ballhandler.

You can make yourself more than twice as effective as a dribbler—using skills you already know. All you have to do is pay special attention to your weak hand.

Watch the next youth league basketball game in your town and see how many baskets are made from the right side. Most likely you won't see any from the left side. This is because most players are right-handed and have not developed left-handed skills.

If you learn to go to your left as well as your right, you'll be unpredictable. And you'll get a bonus: burn a defender to the left a couple of times, and all those overplays to the right you keep seeing will disappear.

Here are some ways to strengthen your left hand:

• **Casual use:** Whenever you handle the ball before and after practice—and on your way to the water fountain during breaks—dribble with your weak hand.

• **Go for 100:** Dribble 100 times with your left hand before practice. Work your way around imaginary defenders or through an obstacle course.

• **Race against yourself:** With a friend timing you, dribble from halfcourt with your strong hand, make a layup, and speed dribble back. Your goal is to do the same thing using your weak hand within one second of your strong-hand time.

• **Beat up the weaklings:** Play a game of one-on-one against someone a few years younger than you. But to make it a fair game, require yourself to play only with your weak hand and make all baskets with that hand.

• **Tale of the tape:** Wrap your little finger and ring finger of your right hand in athletic tape. This makes it more difficult to dribble with that hand. Just as important, it will give you an awareness to use your left hand when possible.

Even when you're not on the basketball court you can develop dexterity with your left hand by using it in such tasks as brushing your teeth and eating. It costs you no time and will give you confidence in your weak hand. In fact, the next game you watch on TV, try working the remote lefty!

Instead of playing an unfair game of one-on-one, bigger players should compete using only the weak hand.

8 THE LONG DRIBBLE

Don't be a standing target. Keep moving downcourt
without a bunch of bounces.

Go somewhere with it.

Dribbling without moving is like drawing a target on your uniform for defenders. You're just giving them more time to move in on you, and you're using up a valuable option with the ball. Even novice players understand that. Still, many of us forget that it's also costly to dribble and not advance downcourt as much as possible. Practicing the long dribble will help you learn to "go somewhere."

Here are ways to train yourself to cover a lot of ground without a lot of bounces.

• **From the foul line extended (the wing):** Practice making layups with only one dribble. Make sure you are not traveling when you first try it, so as not to develop a bad habit. Keep your eyes on the basket for your layups; this isn't a time to get sloppy about making them.

• **From halfcourt:** Use three dribbles for a layup. You'll have to really push hard and extend; after four or five drives you'll be winded.

This exercise gives you the confidence to explode to the basket in a dribble or two. After awhile, add a defender starting right next to you. You'll see that you can go almost as fast dribbling as the defender without the ball alongside you.

It's especially difficult to long dribble with your weak hand if you haven't practiced it; make sure to keep your hand on top of the ball, and practice keeping the ball away from the defense.

An extra benefit to long-dribble practice is conditioning. You'll train your body to handle more quick bursts, and get used to handling the ball when you're tired.

Try making a layup from the wing using just one dribble.

9 TWO-BALL DRILL

Reinforce a dribbling fundamental: do it by feel rather than by sight.

A playground showoff maneuver that actually makes you a better player is the two-ball drill. If you can dribble a ball well with each hand, you're showing that a defender can't overplay you to your strong hand.

Learn to bounce both balls at the same time, then learn to dribble them alternately. Then learn to dribble two balls while running and maneuvering. If your weak hand can control it as well as your strong, you're twice as hard to guard.

The two-ball dribble also reinforces a dribbling basic: it's a touch skill, not a visual one. You'll only be able to look at one ball at a time, which means the other hand is dribbling solely by feel.

Remember, a good way to see if you have the right feel for the ball is to check your hand after dribbling. The palm should be clean—after all, no basketball maneuver involves touching the ball with your palms. The fingers should have their share of dirt, especially at the fingertips. If the upper palm and lower thumb area have some dirt, that's OK. These areas often receive a bounced ball, especially if you're on the run. They serve as cushions as the dribble is rotated over to the fingertips.

When you finish a day of play, including practicing your two-ball dribbling, check both hands. If the right has plenty of wear and the left doesn't, you'll know that you're a predictable dribbler.

Two-ball dribbling calls for coordination and skill with both hands. The player on the left is dribbling too high and his body is too rigid. The player on the right has better ball and body positioning.

10 MARAVICH DRILLS

Beyond his hotdog play, the NBA's Pete Maravich was a skilled ballhandler. Here's how he did it—all by himself.

His style of play was years ahead of its time. He would throw crazy passes and wear floppy socks. We'd copy him, and it drove our coaches crazy.

But Pistol Pete Maravich made sure he had the skills necessary to be the NBA's first—and ultimate—hotdog.

Maravich, the NCAA's all-time leading scorer with 44.2 points per game at Louisiana State University from 1967 to 1970, worked hard at his ballhandling skills. He worked so hard that there's a ballhandling sequence known as the Maravich drills. Every day after practicing with his team, he would work by himself. The drills developed excellent coordination and quickness as well as strength and endurance in his arms and hands.

He did the following 10 times each:

• **Ball slaps:** Holding the ball in front of your chest, slap it hard as you move it from hand to hand.

• **Pinches:** Holding the ball in your right hand, *pinch* it toward your left, using all five fingers. The ball will squirt from one hand to another. Go back and forth.

• **Taps:** Hold the ball over your head with arms fully extended. Tap the ball back and forth between your fingertips.

• **Circles:** Pass the ball around your head 10 times; then around your waist; then around each leg. Keep your head up, if you can, so you're handling the ball totally by feel.

• **Figure-eight passing:** Hold the ball at knee level. Keep your feet stationary and apart. Pass the ball in and out of your legs in a figure-eight motion.

• **Drops:** Hold the ball in front of your legs with your left hand in front and right hand in back. Without letting the ball hit the floor, quickly switch the position of your hands. Repeat quickly.

- **One-hand dribbles:** Using only your right hand, dribble the ball around your right foot. Then do left-hand, left-foot. Remember to keep your head up and dribble with only your fingertips.

- **Figure-eight dribbles:** Dribble in and out of your legs in a figure eight.

- **Four-point spider dribbles:** Stand stationary with your feet apart. Bounce the ball once in front of your legs with the left hand, once with the right hand, once reaching behind and through your legs with the left, and once in back with the right. Keep the ball low and between your legs.

Maravich often upset his NBA coaches with his fancy plays. But he completed most of them because he developed such exceptional hand quickness and strength. He demonstrated the beauty of basketball: you don't need anyone else to make you a better player. All you need is a ball and a patch of concrete.

Pass the ball in a figure eight through your legs while keeping your head up. This forces you to handle the ball totally by feel.

11 SPIN TO WIN

A change of direction turns off a defender.

If you're in the open court and the defender has your path to the basket cut off, a spin dribble could be valuable. The spin allows you to change directions without switching hands in front of your body. It helps you keep the ball away from the defender the whole time, but the trade-off is that you momentarily can't see the basket or cutting teammates.

To execute a spin, dribble hard with your right hand toward the defender, then stop with your left foot forward and planted. The ball should be back by your right foot. Then make a 270-degree back pivot off your left foot, and you're headed to the left of the defender.

Make sure you pull the ball close to your body with your right hand as you complete the pivot. Your final right-hand dribble is a quick one—keep the ball at knee level or below—as your left hand takes over. Make your first step after the pivot with your right foot. That seals off the defender from leaning in and poking the ball away from your left hand.

Watch out for other defenders reading your spin and double-teaming you in your blind spot. Once you've started a spin, it's difficult to change your mind.

From the left side, it's a left-hand dribble and a right-foot pivot. After you make the move, you'll be going to the right of the defender.

Baseline players can use the spin dribble well because the defense is trained to defend the baseline at all costs. So when a dribble down the right baseline is cut off, a quick spin will get you open for a second or two. From there, you're often only one dribble away from a layup.

Practice the spin dribble at walking speed first, maybe even without the ball. The footwork of planting the opposite foot and then pivoting is essential.

Because going too quickly on a spin move can throw you off-balance, this is a good move to practice by making a layup. Start from either corner, dribble the ball along the baseline, make a quick spin, and complete the shot. By mastering the layup at the end, you'll have added another offensive move to your game and will be confident to use it in competition.

To spin left, plant your left foot, then make a 270-degree pivot away from your defender.

12 RETREATING AND CHANGING PACE

There is a way around the defense: make a quick retreat.

Some defenses are designed to get you to pick up your dribble. The thinking is that once you pick up the ball while coming down the court, you have to pass it to someone, and that gives the defense a steal opportunity.

To keep your dribble while there's trouble all around, practice the retreat dribble. That is, learn to dribble while running backward. At the least, you'll make the defense cover more ground; and often the defense will stop chasing you and you can easily maintain your dribble.

When you see a double-team coming, push off your front foot and move backward with your rear foot. It's a slide-step movement.

Once you get the defense spaced out, consider attacking again or dumping the ball off to a teammate. Of course, to make this decision you need to see the whole floor, so keeping your head up while retreating is a must. After all, the situation on the court is about to change, and you can't evaluate it if you can't see it.

The best way to practice the retreat dribble is to mix it in with your other dribbling practices. Start at one baseline and dribble four times forward, then quickly retreat for two dribbles. Cross the ball over to your other hand (more on crossovers later) and go four forward, two retreat, with the other hand. Keep it up until you reach the other baseline.

A more aggressive way to trick the defense is with the change-of-pace dribble. Its purpose is to make a defender believe you're slowing down. When he relaxes, you take the ball to the basket. When you slow down, plant your front foot, straighten up slightly, and throw your head up. Many defenders will instinctively straighten up, too. That's when you've got 'em. Accelerate quickly by pushing off your lead foot, use a low dribble, and head to the basket.

Learn to dribble going backward as well as forward. The threat of retreating gives the defense another direction to think about.

13 CROSSOVER DRIBBLE

A handy, but difficult, maneuver to get by your defender.

Even before the referees relaxed the palming rule, the crossover was the most popular way to sharply change direction and beat a defender on a drive to the basket.

Unlike the spin, players are able to see the basket during this move—which means it's easier to dump the ball off if a double-team appears. The crossover lets dribblers use their momentum toward the basket to their advantage; it's just a weight shift, and a move to the right becomes a move to the left.

The crossover works especially well when a defender has you overplayed, but be careful: the danger is that the defender might be able to tip the ball away if you're being guarded too closely.

Presuming you're being overplayed to the right, push off hard toward your left foot and force the ball across your body on a diagonal path. Receive the ball with your left hand on a short hop. Let your left hand *give* a little, going upward to soften the force of the hard diagonal dribble. Then it's a long crossover step with your right foot and you're on your way to the basket. Your body positioning prevents the ball from being stolen.

Two cautions:

1. Don't reach across for the ball with your left hand; let the ball come to your left side. Reaching over exposes the ball to the defender, and often you'll pull back and dribble the ball off your foot.

2. As the ball goes from right to left, it will tend to pick up topspin, and could bounce low and away from you. Put a little backspin on the crossover dribble to make sure the ball comes up at a less severe angle.

Crossover moves that a few years ago were considered carrying violations are now legal. But don't get too caught up in copying Kobe Bryant or Allen Iverson. Their high dribbles aren't really part of the crossover; they are just distracting the defense to set up the quick diagonal dribble. Their real move, which they do very well, is the hard exchange from right to left and explosive first step to the basket afterward.

Set your defender up with a move in one direction, then go past him.

14 BEHIND THE BACK/BETWEEN THE LEGS

Two high-risk moves that work in the right time and place.

The score has never changed because a player dribbled behind his back. Or through his legs. Still, young players somehow put as much emphasis on looking good as helping their team score.

This is especially true in playground games. Point guards will walk the ball downcourt, dribbling the ball around their body, even though there is no defender to beat. *After all, everyone's looking at me.*

Get over it!

The sad part is, both moves have their place in going around defenders who are overplaying you. Use them in one-on-one situations only; both moves are high-risk and are excellent targets for double-teams.

- **Behind-the-back dribble:** This works best when going from your strong hand to your weak one. If your path to the right is blocked and you don't want to cross the ball over in front of the defense, simply step forward with your left foot and exchange the ball from your right to the area where your left foot was. Think of it as a stationary yo-yo, and you want the ball to go in a perfect V shape. Be careful not to wrap the ball around your body too much; doing that gives your dribble topspin, and you'd better be on the run or else you won't catch up with it.

- **Between-the-legs dribble:** Use this as another alternative to the crossover. Ideally, you push the ball with a hard dribble with your right hand, making the defender think you're going to stop. You have to tempt him with the ball a little bit; when he lunges, push it through your legs from right to left and quickly step past the lunger. When executed perfectly, the defender will slap and miss just above your knee as you're dribbling by.

A lot of players will try to hypnotize the defender with constant between-the-legs dribbles. This works only if the defender isn't very good. Generally, all that happens is the rest of the defense gets more time to move over and help, and a double-team develops.

The final reason not to show off your moves for no reason is a competitive one: simply don't let your opponent know that those moves are part of your game until you need them. Then you have the element of surprise on your side.

The most vulnerable point: it's difficult to change your move when the ball is behind your leg.

15 DRIBBLING BY YOURSELF

*Nobody to play with? That's OK. A ball, some props,
and a little imagination can go a long way
to making you a better player.*

If you push yourself to be a better dribbler, you will be. And you can even invent some opponents. You can use chairs, bowling pins, even orange cones to practice dribbling moves. Just set them up in a line.

First, practice your straight crossover move. Dribble up to each cone and shift the ball from one hand to the other. Remember to make the crossover dribble a quick one.

Then space the cones out a little more and practice your spins. Spin right to left, then approach the next cone with your left-hand dribble and make a left-to-right spin. Learning to do successive spins quickly sometimes has more pressure to it than making just one such move in a game. That overtraining will force you to cement your technique.

Start racing against yourself. See how long it takes you to weave through the cones 10 times without stopping. Write down your best time on your calendar. If you practice enough, you'll have your improvement documented as you go.

Another way to develop your dribbling skills is to practice with your eyes closed. Start off dribbling stationary for about 30 seconds. (Have someone else time you, so you don't have to peek.) Then add in eyes-closed dribbling with alternate hands. Once you get that down, make some pretend moves and vary the cadence of your dribbles, like in a real game.

Just make sure you don't practice eyes-closed dribbling from an upright position; that's not how games are. Keep your knees bent and your back straight.

Use cones to provide defense when there isn't any around.

16 SEATED BALLHANDLING

Give your legs a rest and your hands a workout with these drills.

Worn out from all that running in practice? There are still ways to improve your ballhandling while sitting down.

- **Typewriter dribbles:** Race your friends or race against the clock while dribbling in a chair. Do 50 low, quick dribbles with your right hand, then quickly convert to the left hand and do 50 more. This will develop more hand strength and power, which will give you better control in tight situations.

- **Chair drop:** Sit forward in a chair with your legs apart, holding the ball with both hands above your knees. Drop the ball between your legs and quickly move both hands behind your knees and catch the ball before it hits the floor. Then flick the ball quickly above your knees, bring your hands back up, and catch it again. Try for 10 drop-and-catches in a row without missing.

- **Around your world:** The idea is to continuously dribble as you maneuver the ball around your body. Sit on the ground and typewriter dribble with your right hand. Rock back, lift both legs up, and "go under the bridge" to switch the ball to your left hand. Lean forward for the behind-the-back switch from left hand to right.

Presuming you have a suitable floor, you can even do all three of these dribbling drills in your house—away from parents—while watching TV. A 30-minute show often has three commercial breaks;

do one drill during each of the two-minute periods of advertisements, and you'll have added another ballhandling workout without missing anything. And keep your eyes on the TV, not the ball, to reinforce that ballhandling is by feel, not by sight.

Drop the ball, quickly swing your hands under your knees, and catch it.

17 DRIBBLING GAMES

Get real: bounce the ball with some defenders in your way.

Practicing dribbling by yourself is great, but in games there's that pesky obstacle known as defense. Fortunately, everyone on the team can get in dribbling practice all at once. You want to practice dribbling while keeping your opposite hand up, keeping defenders from reaching in and poking the ball away.

• **Dribble war:** Two dribblers compete against each other, each trying to knock the other's ball away. On a regulation court, use the center circle or a foul-line circle as the boundaries. Players should get used to minor bumping, because that will happen in game situations. In addition, dribble war requires a crouched position with heads up. The winner is whoever knocks the ball away from the other player.

• **Dribble tag:** With five to eight dribblers, use the three-point circle and the end line to create boundaries. One person starts off as *it* and, while dribbling, tries to tag the other players. Everyone is inside the circle. Those who commit dribbling violations or go out of bounds are automatically *it* because they essentially have committed turnovers. Another way to play dribble tag is to have *it* chase down all the players and tag them out. Players take turns being *it*, and whoever tags out everyone else in the shortest time is the winner.

• **One-on-two dribbling:** If you have two partners, take turns trying to get from one end of the court to the other against a double-team. This kind of dribbling is discouraged in games, but is a great way to practice. You'll find yourself quicker and nimbler.

All three of these exercises discourage the "go-nowhere" dribble that surfaces when players are bouncing the ball just because it's in their hands and they feel they must do something with it.

Dribble war helps improve ballhandling and ball protection. Try to knock the ball away from your opponent.

PASSING

18 "NICE PASS"

Players who master passing the ball can expect a lot in return.

"Nice pass!"

It's probably the best compliment a player receives on the basketball court. It usually means that your teammate has scored. And often it means you'll get a nice pass back sometime. Good, unselfish passing is like a smile; you can't help but reciprocate.

The key to good passing is simplicity. A good pass is easily handled and isn't forced. It's usually 12 to 18 feet (the longer ones can be intercepted) and is made with control.

Younger players can get into trouble copying the one-handed passes the pros make. A 6-foot-6 NBA player has hands that can devour a basketball; a 5-foot grade-schooler does not. With two hands you can "pull the string" on a pass you suddenly decide not to make because your receiver has become covered.

As with dribbling, getting fancy is a disturbing problem with passing. More often than not a fancy pass will fool your teammate as well as the defense. And it becomes contagious. If one player completes a behind-the-back pass, you can bet the other four players on the court will be looking for an opportunity to throw one.

The best players have mastered a variety of passes. This makes them more unpredictable and helps their teammates get better shots. Good passers also have the ability to see the whole court, not just part of it. That's why most of the time players earn a "good pass" praise; it's because they've had their heads up, correctly analyzed what was happening on the floor, and made the right decision. Throwing the ball was the easy part!

Learn to throw your passes fundamentally perfect so you won't have to think about them during the game. This will also help you to deliver passes more quickly, before the defense has time to react.

Good passing becomes contagious within a team.

19 CHEST PASS

It's a pass of efficiency.

The chest pass is the most efficient way to move the ball. It's what you use to get the ball to a teammate quickly when there is no defender in the way.

Begin with the ball close to your chest. Push the ball ahead, snapping your wrists so that your hands turn inside out. When you finish, your thumbs should be down and the tops of your hands should face each other. You want to hit your teammate in the chest, or at whatever target is given.

How hard do you throw it? That depends on the situation. If your teammate is only about 10 feet away and isn't an experienced player, you have to let up a little bit, putting a little bit of *loop* on the ball. (Coaches say "Get some air under it.") But for most situations the ball should be passed on a line—that's the quickest way to get it from your hands to your teammate's.

When you practice your passing, make sure your first movement is a forward push, not a windup. Cocking your hands before you pass takes time, and gives the defense more time to cover your target.

Players should step forward when there is time, but passing without stepping is quicker. Just remember that you lose power by not stepping.

Finish a chest pass with your thumbs down. Your fingertips are the last part of your hand to touch the ball.

20 BOUNCE PASS

A handy way to get the ball by a defender.

Not many defenders can touch the floor quickly to deflect a ball, which is why the bounce pass is so valuable. If you're in trouble with the ball or want to slip a pass by the defense to a teammate who can score, sometimes the bounce pass is the best option. It forces the defender to get in an unnatural position, tilting his torso so his hand can get near the floor as a ball is whizzing by.

The beautiful thing about a bounce pass in basketball is that it's so natural: a perfectly round ball will always bounce true. And it's easy to handle: the floor takes a lot of the zip off the ball, so bad-hands players love it.

To throw the bounce pass, push the ball from your chest as you would for a chest pass, but aim at a target on the floor about two-thirds of the way to your receiver. The most common flaw is failing to aim close enough to the receiver—the ball takes a long hop, then *dies* into the hands of a streaking defender.

The ball should bounce up around the receiver's waist. Your hand action makes the bounce pass more reliable: start with your thumbs up on the pass and finish by pushing your fingers all the way through, the thumbs face the floor. That hand movement gives the bounce pass more backspin and increases the angle of the pass, making it easier to handle.

Take a small step in the direction of each pass. This gives you more power. Keep your eyes on your target and make sure your fingertips are the last thing to touch the ball.

The difficult part is knowing when to throw a bounce pass and when a regular chest pass will do. Watch a good college game and see how the guards are programmed to make the right kind of pass.

• **Bounce pass:** Throw to teammates cutting for a layup, beating a defender backdoor, or to those who aren't blessed with good hands. In each case, you're trading the speed of a pass in the air for the flexibility a receiver has in snagging a bouncing ball.

• **Air pass:** Throw to a big man under the basket if it looks like a double-team is coming; throw it in traffic to those with good hands and when ball movement is the most important thing. The trade-off here is that there are 10 defenders' arms that are comfortable snatching passes anywhere from 3 to 7 feet above the floor—the primo chest pass zone.

A final word about bounce passes: it looks pretty to throw those one-handers with topspin or fancy spinning curveballs, but try to resist. Unless it's a soft underhand spin, they often bring more turnovers than good plays.

The ball should bounce about two-thirds of the way to the receiver.

21 OVERHEAD PASS

A pass to use when the defense is in the way.

If you're going to learn only one pass, make it the overhead pass. Throw a chest pass with a defender in your face? You can't. Throw a bounce pass in a halfcourt offense? Five defenders can cover a lot of ground by the time the ball bounces to the floor and back up on the way to a receiver.

Let's look at the situations when an overhead pass is the best pass:

- Feeding the inside players (except when you're passing from the baseline)

- Inbounding the ball with a defender in front of you

- Getting off an outlet pass after a rebound

To throw an overhead pass properly, hold the ball equally with your hands above your head. Snap your wrists, pointing all fingers at your target. You want to step toward your target to generate more power, but sometimes against an extremely sticky defense that's not possible. In those cases, at least make sure you're not falling backward, which would cause the ball to float for an interception.

Overhead passes are especially important to boys' and girls' teams around age 10. The players still don't have the concept of staying spaced apart, so chest passes that are routinely open at the older level just bounce off a swarm of defenders' arms. But many of those players don't have the arm strength or ability to get the ball up above the head, and many children haven't developed the hands to catch the ball up high. The only way to improve that? Practice. (Sorry, no magic potions.)

The pass is meant to be caught at chin level or above. If it's a high-to-low pass, bearing in on the receiver's waist, it handcuffs him. Like a crossed-up wide receiver in football, the player doesn't know whether to catch the ball with the thumbs up or thumbs down.

Practice the overhead pass whenever you pass to your teammates during shooting drills. If there's no defender in front of you, pretend there is one. And put in a good ball fake to give you a little more room to pass.

Your teammates will thank you for it.

The overhead pass is good for feeding post players.

22 BASEBALL PASS

Keep it under control, and watch your pivot foot.

A professional outfielder can throw the ball 300 feet, but the longest pass you'll need for basketball is about 60 feet. So even though we're using a much bigger ball, we'll sacrifice a lot of distance for accuracy. Remember, unlike baseball, in basketball there's a defense to contest the pass.

Getting your feet in the right position is the most important part of throwing a baseball pass. Heaving a large ball with just one hand is an unnatural motion, and if your body is out of control the ball will curve. The goal is for the ball to go straight.

Try to get your feet parallel to the sideline for the pass, and, without traveling, shift your weight from your back foot to your front and throw.

The follow-through is what keeps the ball on-line. Finish with your thumb pointing toward the ground. If you don't, you're looking at an unintentional curveball.

Practice throwing the baseball pass to a stationary teammate first, then try throwing to moving targets.

Because you have to make your right (back) foot your pivot foot instead of your usual left, the baseball pass requires decisiveness. If you pull down a rebound and go into a triple threat, it's difficult to then adjust your body for a baseball pass to a streaking teammate. Often that change in decisions will cause shuffling feet, and a travel.

Be aware of the abilities of your receiver, because the passer-receiver angle can be tricky. If the target is running directly away from the ball, judging the speed and distance of the throw isn't easy. But, if your receiver is running toward the pass, he will be able to see it more easily but will have trouble adjusting if the ball is thrown off-line.

Although the baseball pass is made with one hand, use the other hand as a guide to maintain control.

23 SIDE PASS (PUSH PASS)

Sometimes it helps to take sides.

When there's a defender in your face—and maybe another one sprinting toward you—it's difficult to throw a two-hand pass. You need to get around your defender and dump the ball quickly. That's where the side pass (or push pass) comes in, but you have to be clever.

It's a very easy pass to throw from triple threat position. Because the defender is smothering you, his arms are active in trying to swat the ball away. Use this to your advantage. Decide whether you're throwing either above or below his arm, and fake the other way. When his arm goes down, throw over it. When his arm goes up, slip a one-handed bounce pass under it. The power comes from your wrist: it's a quick flip, because you don't have time for a windup.

For better control, keep your fingers up and your elbow down. An underhanded flip of more than a couple feet is very hard to control, and once your arm motion has started you can't pull the ball back.

Because you're throwing the ball with only one hand, make sure you have enough power. A pass from your shoulders that dives down to your teammate's waist is hard to handle because players don't know whether to catch the ball with their fingers up or down. Save them from having to make that decision.

Learn to throw the side pass both left- and right-handed. Accuracy is especially a problem when passing with your weak hand, because the ball can easily "tail" away from the target or quickly hook away.

Practice throwing the ball against a wall with your weak hand during breaks in practice, and whenever you're getting the balls out to start practice. (Some coaches require weak-hand use on all *casual* touches of the basketball, like getting out balls to start a drill or putting them away at the end of practice. Be ahead of your coach: impose that rule on yourself to be a better player.)

Most teams don't practice the side pass because it doesn't look as fundamentally pretty as a two-hand pass. But against swarming defenses, you'll have to use it.

The side pass comes in handy when you're closely guarded.

24 BEHIND-THE-BACK PASS

If you get fancy, make it work. Or else.

Here are my rules when it comes to passing:

• If a player makes a bad chest, overhead, or bounce pass and we turn the ball over, I don't take him out. I figure he's making an effort to get the ball to a teammate, and mistakes while trying to do that are acceptable.

• If a player turns the ball over with a behind-the-back pass when he could have used something else, he comes out.

• If he throws a behind-the-back pass and it helps us get a good shot, I keep my mouth closed and he stays in.

The players hear my rules before our first game, and I explain the logic:

We're playing this game to affect the scoreboard, not the highlight film. (In fact, after coaching for 10 years at various levels I cannot remember seeing a TV camera even once!) The players know that games are not the time for experimentation.

Having said that, I acknowledge that there are rare times when a behind-the-back pass could be effective. Coaches approve of it in two-on-one fast-break situations. If you're driving to the basket with the ball on your right hip, you may either lay it in or, if the defender lunges at you, slip it behind your back to a wide-open teammate.

So if you're throwing it, do it right.

Cup the ball in your throwing hand and swing your arm in a circular path around the body and behind the back. The power comes from your arm and fingers, not from turning your shoulders. If you turn your shoulders, you give away that you're throwing a behind-the-back pass, and by the time the ball gets all the way around your body the defense has had a long time to cut in front of your target.

Practice throwing the behind-the-back pass off a wall about 10 feet in front of you. If you can get the ball to bounce straight back to you, you're really whipping the ball hard. To make the pass to your side instead of your front, let up a little bit on the arm whip.

And make sure your teammates know that the behind-the-back pass is in your repertoire. Otherwise, you'll fake them out as well as the defense.

The behind-the-back pass is a way to slip the ball to your teammate in a two-on-one fast break.

25 TWO-BALL PASSING DRILL

Take the boredom out of throwing the ball back and forth.

Every team drills on passing fundamentals by having players face each other and throw the ball back and forth. This works the first couple of practices, but after awhile it becomes, well, boring. There's no defense, no urgency to move the ball. And when in a game are both players that stationary, with nothing else to think about?

A good way to test passing technique is the two-ball drill. Two players pass two basketballs back and forth, using different types of balls. For example, the striped ball is the *bounce pass* ball and the leather one is the *overhead*.

Try to go for one minute without a bad pass or a drop. Any mistakes in form, such as failing to step into the ball or throwing weak bounce passes, will surface because of the pressure of trying to keep two basketballs going.

Just as important, the two-ball passing drill provides a mental test. As the final seconds of the timed period close in, the passers are imploring each other to keep going faster and faster—and must remember which ball is the *overhead* and which ball is the *bounce pass*. So concentration and quick thinking get a workout, too.

After a two-ball workout with bounce passes and overhead passes, go on to the side pass. Throw from your right hand to the receiver's left. Your partner will do the same. And remember to drill with your left hand, too, keeping your arm above your waist and throwing the side pass overhand, even when your arms are tired.

This is also a great drill for a parent and a child, because instead of competing against your child, you are working with him.

The two-ball passing drill develops quickness and coordination. Use two types of basketballs: one goes high, the other goes low.

26 BULL IN THE RING

Have fun while working on basic passing skills.

To really sharpen your passing, you need to practice against a defense. But you don't have to play a game. We often play *bull in the ring* because it forces players to decide which pass to throw, where to throw it, and how to handle a defender. It takes at least six players. Here's how you play:

Form a 15-foot circle with five passers, and put a sixth player (the *bull*) in the center of the ring. As the players around the circle throw to each other, the player in the center tries to steal the passes. (A passer can't throw to the person immediately next to him—that's too easy, and unfair to the defender.)

For 30 seconds the passers work the ball around, counting aloud each pass they complete. The defender has to run at the passers. If he intercepts a pass, he holds the ball for 5 seconds. If a receiver drops a pass, it's a free ball, and the defender can grab it, again holding it for 5 seconds. At the end of the 30 seconds, the defender has to do a pushup for each pass completed. (Use jumping jacks for younger players.)

If you have eight or nine players, it's fun to go with two bulls. This is even more realistic for the passers, and there's the added benefit of two players working on their defensive communication.

This competition reinforces many passing fundamentals: move the ball quickly, use ball fakes, and think clearly while under pressure. It also discourages *float* passes because they eat up valuable time.

Just as important, it gets teammates passing to each other and helps them get used to each other. And the game doesn't require a hoop, so you can play it outside if your gym time is limited.

¡Olé!

Practice passing with a defender chasing after the ball.

27 BALL FAKES

Fooling around has its advantages.

Aggressive defenders can't help it. If it looks like they can get an interception, they'll shift their weight in preparation to go for the steal. You can take advantage of that by using ball fakes.

Defenders who can't see both the passer and the receiver are especially vulnerable to ball fakes. If you start to pass and the defender bites, a quick cut by your teammate will put the defender way out of position.

Ball fakes on your defender make you a better passer. You can get yourself more room to throw an overhead by breaking down your defender with a good ball fake. Think "Fake low, throw high." The defender has to react to your fake and will make himself shorter, creating more distance for you. Then throw the overhead pass directly over the head of your defender. (Give him a haircut!) That's the least likely place for a deflection, because arms weren't created with bending to the top of one's head in mind, and that's a long way for an arm to go. It's an unnatural position. Try it.

If the player is jumping or is too tall and you can't throw over his head, try to throw directly past his ear. It's the same principle: his arms have a long way to go to reach his ears.

A good ball fake means a big difference for a three-point shooter, too. Imagine you're the point guard, attacking the middle of a zone. By faking a pass to someone under the basket, the bottom defenders on the zone have to react. If you have a good shooter in the corner, nobody is left to guard him. And having plenty of time is vital to successful three-point shooting.

When running offensive patterns, each player should make at least one ball fake before passing. This is how games go, because good defenders can sniff out where the ball is supposed to be passed, so throwing it there would result in a turnover.

You can beat a lesser team by pure physicality; that is, being bigger, faster, and stronger. But sometimes you'll play teams with better physical skills than yours. Fake well to neutralize that advantage.

To get room to throw an overhead pass, say to yourself "fake low, throw high."

28 PASSER-RECEIVER COMMUNICATION

Know what your teammates are going to do before your opponents figure it out.

Basketball is improvisational. One player sees another cutting toward the basket and, through years of learned experience, throws the ball right where the teammate can get an easy layup. The difficult part of that pass wasn't necessarily the *how,* it was the *when.*

To quickly establish good rapport with another player, do the following:

• **Have the receiver direct traffic:** Two players stand 12 to 18 feet apart. The catcher simply puts up his hands where he wants the ball thrown. It can be above his head, at his knees, to his left, or to his right. The passer uses different moves and different types of passes to get him the ball.

After a few passes with obvious signals, it's time to be a little more coy. This time, the receiver motions with his head, eyes, or body, as though he is posting up a defender. Again, the passer must deliver the ball where requested.

• **Have the passer direct traffic:** At first, the passer simply points where he's going to throw the ball. The receiver must respond. After that, the passer uses the same coy tricks: he can gesture with his head, eyes, or body. The receiver will position himself to receive the pass.

While passers and receivers are getting to know each other, practice the fake-shot pass. The player with the ball goes up as if to shoot, but uses that shooting motion to dump the ball off to someone closer to the basket. The fake-shot pass can be effective, but sometimes too effective. The receiver sometimes will turn around to anticipate the rebound, and the ball will sail out of bounds.

That's why it's good early in the season for passers and receivers to get a look at what their teammates' fake-shots look like. After all, they're the ones who stand to benefit.

In practice, point to the spot where you'll throw the ball.

29 MARINE BASKETBALL

The military's contribution:
a game in which no dribbling is allowed.

Imagine loving the game so much that you would play it even on sand. That's what a group of Marines did in the 1960s on a beach in San Diego. Little did they know that "Marine basketball" would become an excellent way to develop passing skills.

The idea is simple. Because you're playing basketball on sand, it's impossible to dribble. No one-on-one drives, no crossovers, no behind-the-back moves. Just passing from one player to another, and a lot of cutting.

I coach teams to play Marine basketball fullcourt, but instead of using five players per team, I use seven. The idea is to pass the ball from one player to another to get a good shot. I allow bounce passes (something the Marines didn't have), but a dribble is a turnover. The other rules of basketball still apply (fouls, traveling, three seconds in the lane, and so on).

Another variation on the game is to award one point each time a team successfully passes the ball into the lane. This encourages you to look for the inside players, who can always quickly pass the ball back out if they don't have a good shot.

There's a halfcourt version of Marine basketball, called *three-on-three, no dribble*. It's just like it sounds, encouraging the players to pass and cut. One dribble can be allowed sometimes because the threat of a drive changes the way a defense positions itself.

For younger teams, Marine basketball can be toned down to good old keep-away. The first team to complete 20 passes against the other team is the winner. This is fun for players early in the season, when they need the idea of *pass first* cemented into their games.

No one knows how many of the pioneers of Marine basketball went on to become outstanding players. But if they ever got called to war, you could be sure their teamwork was stellar.

To improve passing, play games in which dribbling is illegal.

4

SHOOTING

30 THE BASICS OF SHOOTING

What it takes to make a basket more often than not.

Shooting is everyone's favorite part of basketball, and for good reason. You let go of the ball, and two seconds later you have a clear result: either you succeed or you don't.

Younger players will still shoot set shots; older ones will shoot jumpers. Either way, learning the basics can help ensure future success.

• **Stance:** Bend your knees slightly and make sure your feet point at the basket. Bent knees help put the right arc on your shot.

• **Shot position:** The ball rests on your fingertips and your wrist is bent back 90 degrees so that you can see a wrinkle at the back of your hand. The ball is at least shoulder height for jump-shooters, lower for younger players.

• **Grip:** You make more shots with your dominant hand. Put your dominant hand in the center of the ball, with the fingers spread comfortably and the palm not touching the ball.

• **Target:** Pick the point on the hoop closest to you. That's better than picking the entire hoop, because it sharpens your focus. Picture the ball settling just over the rim and making that distinctive swishing sound.

• **Release:** Thrust your fingers up and forward toward the basket. Think of the word *arc*, or pretend like you're in a telephone booth and the only way to get the ball out is through the top. A good rule for 15-foot shots is to arc the ball 3 or 4 feet above the basket. From in close, 1 or 2 feet is OK.

• **Follow-through:** Picture putting your fingers in the basket. Your fingers are pointing downward after you've released the ball. Leave your hand up there for at least a second to make sure you don't prematurely pull it back.

• **Balance:** Feel your body going slightly toward the basket, feeling a slight forward tilt. If it's a jump shot, you're landing on both feet at the same time, ready to go forward if the ball is short and is caroming back to you off the front rim.

Imagine you're putting your fingers in the basket. Your arm makes a 60-degree angle with your ear.

31 LAYUP BASICS

The easiest shot in basketball is harder than it looks.

The pros and the TV announcers call it *finishing*. Everybody else calls it *making a layup*.

It's supposed to be the easiest shot in basketball, but for some reason, players miss far too many layups. Most of the misses come from a lack of concentration or a feeling of relief that a play has worked and has resulted in an easy shot.

A few pointers on how to make a layup:

• Make sure your eyes remain on the white square on the backboard, even (especially!) while the defense is bearing down on you. Watch on TV: the great players keep their gaze fixed there even while being knocked down.

• For a right-handed layup, jump off your left foot; for a left-handed one, it's your right foot. This gives you maximum height and best shields you from the defense. Training tip: rent a beginning aerobics tape and practice jumping.

• Shoot with your palm facing the basket. Finger rolls look pretty in practice, but they are too hard to control going full steam against a defender. An underhand layup isn't really a shot; it's a throw.

• Jump up, not out. All that broad-jump distance doesn't get you closer to the rim. Players younger than high school should make their final leap inside the painted block. High-schoolers should take off from the block.

• Practice shooting difficult layups, too. Most teams expect you to shoot with the right hand on the right side and left from the left side. So if you're defended that way, you may have to take a left-handed layup on the right because that's what the defense gives you.

Once you get the basics down, it's important to learn to make layups at game speed. To practice, dribble in from the foul line, make your layup, and circle back to the foul line to start another layup. See how many you can make in a minute. By fourth grade or so, it's time to begin practicing with both the right and left hand.

And when you grow to 6-foot-6 or develop a 42-inch vertical leap, you can apply these same principles to dunking.

When shooting a layup, make sure your eyes remain on the white square on the backboard.

32 SHOULDERS SQUARE, OFF TWO FEET

A few lessons in geometry can improve your layup percentage.

To really keep the defense away on your layups is a matter of geometry. Your shoulders must be parallel to the basket. If they're not, the defender can inch closer to you. When you go in for a layup, the ball should be on your outside hip. That way the defender can't get to it.

As you get closer to the basket on your drive, think of bringing your left hand over to meet the right. Don't give in to the urge to be creative and sweep the ball into your defender—you'll get stripped more often than not.

Another benefit of keeping your shoulders parallel is that it trains you to use the backboard. Practice shooting all your close-in shots off the board; that way you're never caught thinking about whether to go for the swish or the bank.

Once you master the one-footed leap for layups, learn to jump off both feet. This gives you better balance in a crowd and allows you to go up strong.

The next time you watch a game on TV, see how many players are able to convert layups for the basket and the foul. Notice how often this is the result of a two-footed jump and a layup. The balance is better, so the typical bump under the basket is negated.

Your feet should be planted firmly before you jump. Visualize yourself stomping your feet through the floor. Use your momentum from your move to the basket to take you up for the layup.

Get your shot up high on the backboard. A lot of beginners, lacking the strength to get the ball all the way up, try to *skim* the ball off the low part of the board and have it skip up, then down into the basket. Instead, the shots should hit high up on the painted square on the backboard and simply fall into the hoop.

A good way to practice going up strong is to involve some defense. With a defender nearby, start dribbling from halfcourt toward the basket. The defender follows one second later, trying to distract you. For the purpose of this exercise, he can run alongside you and yell, but can't jump to block the shot.

The dribbler goes straight to the basket, slows slightly with a two-footed stomp, then keeps his eye on the hoop and makes the layup.

Keep the defender on your hip farthest away from the ball.

33 MIKAN DRILL

Everyone can benefit from big-man skills, but it's no small feat to play well under the basket.

He was the first successful big man, so there's good reason the most famous layup drill is named after him.

George Mikan, all 6 feet 10 inches of him, led the NBA in scoring for six straight years after entering the league in 1949. His size was unheard of during that time, yes, but size alone doesn't put the ball in the basket. Coordination and footwork are essential to playing well near the hoop.

That's what the Mikan drill develops. Decades ago, coaches studied Mikan's skills because they wanted their big men to play like him. So they copied what he did to be successful and made their players practice it.

Start on the right side of the basket about two feet away and bank the ball into the basket. Then, without letting the ball hit the ground, quickly shift over to the left side and make a two-footer from there. Again catch the ball before it hits the ground, shift back to the right side, and convert that basket again.

A beginner should strive to make 10 baskets in a row. A potential high-school player should go for 20. And the more advanced players should not only keep the ball from touching the ground, but should never let the ball drop below eye level. This is logical big-man play, because in games you don't want those pesky guards being able to reach in and poke the ball away. Learn to keep it up high in practice, so in games you won't have to think about it.

If you have a friend to compete with, see how many each of you make in 30 seconds. Make it a disqualification if the ball touches the ground or the player travels.

Keep the ball above your head; try to make 10 in a row, and eventually 20.

34 CORRECTING MISSES

The long and the short of it: some common reasons why shots don't go through the net.

You can miss a shot four ways: to the right, to the left, long, or short. Of these, more than half of misses are short. Don't believe it? Sit down with a notepad and keep track during a televised game. You'll notice that even the best college and pro players have the same shooting faults.

Here are the three main reasons shots fall short:

1. **Stopping the hand:** Proper follow-through is a must. A great finish has the fingers pointing toward the floor. The complete motion: start your shot with your hand back almost parallel to the floor and release while pointing your index finger toward the basket.

2. **Shooting straight-legged:** Like most sports, basketball relies on the legs for power. When you start your shot, your knees must be bent. A shallow knee bend cuts down on power, making for shots with poor arc that are usually short.

3. **Falling away:** This also saps power. Sometimes fallaways work for shots inside of 10 feet, but for anything longer few players consistently get proper arc and distance when not heading toward the basket (one exception: the Heat's Tim Hardaway).

As fundamentals improve, players must learn to shoot under varying degrees of pressure. Players who practice only at half speed will panic when they shoot in a game. That's why all shooting drills should involve some kind of competition.

The simplest drill is for a parent to rebound for a child for a minute. Offer a reward for, say, six baskets in that minute. Raise the stakes accordingly for the skill of the player. And make it fun when you can. Often children develop bad habits by shooting at too-high baskets. The proper height is no more than 1 foot high per year of age (for example, a 7-foot basket for a seven-year-old).

Remember to follow through, bend your knees, and jump slightly toward the basket.

Alignment, release, and follow-through are vital.

35 LEVERS

Locking in your shot, and understanding the mechanics, will improve form.

A physics teacher would love analyzing a basketball shot, because basically it's four levers at work. From the bottom up, the levers are the foot, the knee, the elbow, and the wrist. When all those levers go from open to closed simultaneously, it has a powerful effect on moving the desired object: the basketball. When levers don't extend properly, that means less power—and a short shot.

Sometimes in a game you'll see a player prepare for his free throws by mimicking his motion. What the good ones are doing is reminding themselves to bend their knees and extend their hand all the way through. When they do that, the ball has no choice in the matter: it has to go forward, and usually into the basket.

The basketball shot is good for geometry teachers, too: the foot, knee, elbow, and wrist must all be on the same plane. That means before you shoot the ball, you must make sure your forearm is going up and down, not side to side. When you hear TV announcers talk about shooters needing to get the elbow in, this is what they mean.

After you lock all your levers, make sure your arm finishes up high. More geometry: remember to finish your shot with your arm at a 60-degree angle with your ear. This puts the right amount of arc on the ball and gives you a better chance for the ball to tumble into the basket off the rim on the rare occasions when it's not a swish. Try holding your arm at that 60-degree angle so you'll know what it feels like.

In order to work on form, not results, sit on the floor with your legs extended. Hold the ball in shooting position, about head high. Extend your arms and the ball to a position where you would normally release it for a shot. Then flick the ball upward, focusing on the use of your fingers and wrists. Catch the ball at your shooting position and flick it again. Do this about 10 to 15 times.

Practicing the seated flick teaches you how it feels to release the ball toward the basket. As a bonus, it develops your finger and wrist strength while enhancing your touch and control of the ball.

The foot, knee, elbow, and wrist all close out during a shot.

36 GROOVING YOUR SHOT

Making baskets from 4 feet out will help you in the long run.

Sometimes making a basket can hurt you, especially when practicing shooting. Young players often will do whatever it takes to heave the ball into the basket. They'll lunge. They'll fire the ball from their hip. They'll twist their body in search of more power—even more if they're shooting at a 10-foot basket.

A couple of swishes then spell trouble, because the young player sees the end result—a basket—but doesn't understand that he is developing a bad habit that will later hurt him. The best way to groove your shot is to practice from 4 feet out.

• Stand in front of the basket, drop the ball on the ground, and let it bounce comfortably into your outstretched hand. Handle the ball with your fingertips, not your palm. If your hand isn't large enough to handle a regulation-size ball, use a smaller ball.

• Next, rotate your hand and wrist so your palm faces the basket. Keep your elbow close to your body and your other hand at your side. Flick the ball at the basket and make sure your hand follows all the way through.

• This short shot should be taken with only your hand and fingers. If you have to twist your body to hoist the ball into the hoop, you either need to move closer or shoot at a lower basket. (Note to those who love the three-pointer: if you can't get the ball to the basket from 4 feet out with one hand, your mechanics from outside the circle are probably in serious trouble.)

Why use just one hand? It cements the idea that the weak hand is just a guide. When you shoot with two hands, the thumb on the weak hand often sneaks in to provide more power.

Check your weak hand after you shoot: the thumb should point back toward your face, and the little finger should be the closest one to the basket. If your left hand finishes with your fingers facing the basket, that means your thumb has invaded, and you're probably shooting shots out of your range.

Practicing from 4 feet doesn't impress many friends. It's not as rewarding as a swish from downtown, and will never make ESPN. But in the long run, it will make you a better shooter.

First, drop the ball and let it bounce into your hand. Then, with the ball on your fingertips, turn your fingers toward the basket, keep your elbow in, and shoot.

37 USE THE AIR VALVE

Every basketball has a cheat sheet: a little dot where you should put your hand.

Did you know that every basketball has a built-in guide? It's almost like a cheat sheet for shooters.

It's called the air valve. Yes, that seemingly meaningless little rubber dot can give you instant guidance.

The air valve is at the center of the basketball. You want your hand at the center of the basketball when shooting. Coincidence? I think not.

When shooting foul shots or when working on your technique, place your index finger behind the air valve. (Some shooters use their middle finger as the guide finger. That's OK, too.) Your hand will be automatically in the center of the ball, which means your shot will be on-line if you do everything else correctly.

To improve your shot, do imaginary shooting with a partner. You don't need a basket. Stand facing each other about 15 feet apart. (This takes off the pressure of having to worry about making the shot and allows you to concentrate on form.) Each time you "shoot," leave your hand up in the air and make sure you have proper follow-through. This habit needs to be developed early so you won't have to think about it during games.

Practicing without a basket also helps you learn to shoot straighter. Twisting the body while shooting is a prime reason for misses to the left and right. To make sure your shot is straight, check your feet after each imaginary shot. They should be pointed directly at your target.

Putting the center of your hand on the air valve helps the ball go straight.

38 THE MIDRANGE JUMPER

Want the defense to respect you as a shooter?
Here's the shot to master.

Dunks and three-pointers make the highlights, but the midrange jump shot wins games.

Since the three-point arc came to high schools (and lower levels of play) more than a decade ago, youngsters have been drawn to the long bomb. Too often players are caught waving their arms in the air so they can launch a three, but the teammate with the ball can't get the proper angle for passing. Three or four simple steps to the basket would have set up an open 12-footer.

Being able to make a midrange jumper will open up your whole game. Because the defense will have to respect your shot, you'll be able to drive to the basket easier. Your three-point percentage will go up because you'll have properly grooved your form.

The best way to practice a midrange jumper is to place a ball at each end of the foul line (called the *elbow*). Practice running to each elbow, lining up your foot closest to the basket before you pivot toward the hoop. As you pick up the ball, line up your body with the basket and let the ball fly. Then run to the other elbow, again pivoting off your inside foot, and shoot from that side.

If you don't have someone rebounding for you, go get your own shot, then toss the ball into the air with backspin so it will plop back into your hands as you square up to the basket.

Regular shooting fundamentals apply. Catch the ball at chin level with your shooting wrist cocked. Make sure you elevate on each shot; a set shot is too difficult to get off in traffic.

Once you're solid from the elbows, spin the ball to yourself from each baseline. Then do the same from the 45-degree angle with the basket (the shooter's angle). Think of that shot as an extension of the layup; shoot the ball up high on the backboard's painted square and watch it drop through the hoop.

When checking out an opponent warming up, I look out for the players who can consistently practice and hit from 12 to 15 feet. If I see a center launching up a three-pointer, I figure he is undisciplined, or scared to go to the basket. If it is a guard, he's often more of a stand-and-shoot player. But the player who can score from midrange will frustrate shot-blockers and will get a lot more respect from pressuring guards.

Some years when my team isn't playing well, I even go so far as to ban the three-pointer. This forces players to go to the basket and look for more makeable shots.

Unless, of course, we're down three with five seconds to go. . . .

Learn to shoot the ball well from 12 to 15 feet and your whole game will open up.

39 THE FREE THROW

Don't let nerves get the best of you.
Visualize yourself sinking the shot, and you will.

It's late in the game and your team has fought for a small lead. You've guarded your man intensely, chased after every rebound, and dashed away from your defender enough times to make a few baskets.

Now, with the game on the line, you must stop playing on instinct.

Instead, you're 15 feet away, unguarded, for a free throw.

You have time to look at the scoreboard to see the importance of your shot. (Just to make sure, the opposing coach has graciously called a timeout to give you time to think. How nice!) This is where your mind takes over. It's human to be nervous; just allow those free-throw nerves to work to your advantage.

Mentally make a movie with yourself as the star. Picture yourself going to the foul line, calmly taking a few dribbles, then swishing your shot through the hoop. Play that movie again with your eyes closed to make it more vivid.

Then give your shoulders a shrug to relax them, take a deep breath, and go make your free throws.

But to have that late-game confidence, you must perfect your form during practice:

• Stay square to the basket with your feet pointed toward the rim. Keep your dominant foot slightly in front.

• Make sure your knees are bent, your shooting elbow is tucked almost against your body, and your shooting hand is directly under the ball. Keep your eyes on the basket. Finish with your heels off the floor and your weight on your toes.

• As your knees straighten, release the ball and follow through with a flick of the wrist. Finish your shot with your biceps at a 60-degree angle with your ear; this high finish helps you put a natural arc on the shot. That proper arc will put a good "bite" on the shot, which gives the ball a much better chance of rattling around and falling through on the rare non-swish occasions.

• Remember general shooting fundamentals. Point your fingers at the basket after your shot. Make sure your strong hand follows through. Use your non-shooting hand as a guide, but don't let it affect the shot.

• Shoot each foul shot the same way—I suggest five dribbles—and say a positive word that gives you confidence. (*Swish* is an excellent one; other shooters use *net* or, of course, *money*.)

• Practice shooting under pressure. My favorite is to play "beat Larry Bird." Each successful free throw gives you one point. Each miss gives Mr. Bird three points. The game is over after 11 points. To win, you have to make more than 75 percent of those shots. For beginning shooters, it can always become "beat Shaquille O'Neal." You get two points for a make, and Shaq gets one for a miss (38 percent is enough to win).

Once your foul shot is perfectly grooved, game-time nerves will decrease.

Swish.

Swish.

First, make a movie in your head in which you swish your free throw. Then keep your eyes glued to the basket and let it fly.

40 THREE-POINTERS

The odds are against this long shot.
But if you know when and how, bomb away.

We love that line.

Walk out to shoot around on a regulation basketball court, and what catches your eye first? It's that arc. Depending on the court, it's anywhere from 19 feet to 23 feet away. Sink one from there, and it's worth more than a dunk.

Be careful: that line is quite the temptation. We pass up closer, better shots for a chance at what Miami Heat coach Pat Riley calls *fool's gold*. His point is that often a team will make a couple of threes early in the game for a quick lead, but once the shooters cool off, there's nothing else established. Like most coaches, he likes the ball to go into the paint first. If nothing's going on down there, then it's OK to pass it out for an open three.

So if you're going to shoot it, at least do it the right way. Here are the proper conditions:

- **You're ready:** Your feet are set and you're not leaning one way. The three-point percentage off passes is much higher than off the dribble for this reason.

- **You can get it there:** Your normal shooting motion must apply, and that especially means getting the right arc on the ball.

- **You're open:** If a defender has a hand in your face—or even is close enough to run at you and get you to pull back your arm after the release—pass it off.

- **Rebounders have a chance:** Because shooting 33 percent of threes is considered good, that presumes 67 percent of shots are rebound opportunities. A three-pointer is a better idea if you have teammates ready to rebound.

• **Right score, right time:** What may be a good shot at one point in the game may be a bad one at another. The time when temptation especially sets in is when a team is down two with a few seconds to play. Tv sports shows have given us the "three-pointer-with-a-pileup-celebration" highlight way too many times. You're better off going for the tie than rushing an off-balance three.

The corners and the top of the key are the highly preferable spots for a three-point attempt. Because of the way the arc is drawn, those shots are as much as two feet shorter. And they're direct-line shots, which make it easier to get your feet and body in line with the basket.

Ready, willing, and open: be selective about which three-pointers you shoot.

41 SHOT SELECTION

Know your best shot: those are the ones to take.
A shot out of your range is just like a turnover.

Shooting is something you can learn by yourself. Knowing *when* to shoot is an element of your game you can add when you play pickup games.

Mature players pass up shots they don't have a good chance of making, and thus have higher shooting percentages. Sure, they improve on technique a little bit, but mainly they are eliminating the times they have to run back on defense hollering "My fault!"

Until you get to college, there's no shot clock. The outside shot is almost always there, and taking a shot out of your range is no different than a turnover. Until you prove in practice that you can make a shot, it's usually best not to try it in games.

• **Right away or not at all:** You think you're open, and the pass comes to you. But you've bobbled the pass. Or you've had to think about whether you're open enough. Here's the rule: anytime you stand there deciding, decide not to shoot. Stopping to think that much destroys your rhythm. Pass the ball off and get yourself back into shooting position.

• **Don't worry about "getting yours":** The four other players have each fired one up there. You feel like it's your turn. So you rush one. Usually it'll be a miss. Basketball is not an equal-opportunity situation. Some players' roles are to be rebounders and passers, too.

• **The one-pass shot:** The point guard brings the ball down, and the first player to catch it shoots it. That's something the defense loves to see. They haven't had to work hard, and all five pairs of eyes are on defending the shooter. It's better to make the defense work. The more they have to move and the more decisions they have to make, the more likely they are to break down. This gives you a second more to shoot. As a bonus, making the defense move boosts teammates' chances for an offensive rebound—not to mention morale.

- **Late in the game, go to the hoop:** Say you're down 10 with two minutes to go. What's the other coach saying? That's right: "Don't foul!" The defense will be passive and you can drive to the hoop. Layups, not three-pointers, are the backbone of great rallies.

If you've caught a bad pass, or have bobbled a pass, it's best not to shoot.

42 SHOOTING GAMES

Simulate pressure situations at practice so it feels like the real thing.

They say pressure makes diamonds, so keep the heat on to make your jump shot a gem. When you're in a game, there will be defense, a crowd, and your jangling nerves. There's really no way to train for shooting under pressure, but playing shooting games will give you some idea of what it's like.

Make your games fun, but have a consequence. Winners get a drink first. Losers have to do pushups. Anything that adds pressure to your games will make you better in the long run.

Here are some of my favorite shooting games:

• **21:** Two teams, usually of two players each, race each other, shooting from the foul line (worth two points) and a one-point layup if the two-pointer goes in. The first team to a total of 21 points wins. I like this game because some passing under pressure is necessary, and players learn to follow their shots. For high-school players, I require the one-point layup to be left-handed.

• **Make 10:** Two-player teams race to see which pair can combine to make 10 15-foot jump shots. Players yell out the number of shot the team just sank on each make.

• **Follow the leader:** One person, the leader, takes his teammates from spot to spot on the floor, where each player gets a shot. The first one to make 10 shots wins. Add conditioning by requiring constant dribbling between shots.

• **Knockout:** A favorite among younger players, this takes two balls and a line of shooters. Starting at the foul line (or the top of the key for older players) the first player shoots. If he makes it, the second person shoots and the first player throws his ball to the third player. But if the first shooter misses, the second player can knock him out by making a basket before the first player. The winner is the one who doesn't get knocked out.

There are probably hundreds more shooting games, each tailored to the skills of the players involved. Make up your own, or alter someone else's.

Playing "21" promotes teamwork and shooting under pressure.

43 PRACTICING THREES IN COMPANY

Get the hang of making three-pointers in practice against some competition.

Your three-point percentage is highest when there's no one else in the gym. And it drops only a little bit warming up around friends. But it nosedives when you're running up and down the court with a defender flying at you.

So if you're going to learn to make three-pointers in games, you must practice them in a way other than by standing still. Here are three shooting games that help the three:

1. **Competitive around-the-world:** This is a killer of a two-player game, but it gets older players in shape. Shooters take three-pointers from nine spots on the floor: the two corners, two wings, each side halfway between the corners and the wings, the top of the key and a few feet on each side of the top of the key.

With one player starting from the left corner and one from the right, the race is on to see who makes all nine first. You can make the game harder by requiring a left-handed layup after all misses, enforcing all dribbling rules, or making shooters go back one spot each time they miss. To raise the stakes, require a lap after each miss from the top of the key.

2. **Make 100:** Take your watch and see how long it takes you to make 100 three-pointers. The next day, try to beat your time. Enforce the no-repeat rule: you have to move to a different spot on the floor following each make.

3. **Shoot and box:** This game requires three players and two basketballs. One player passes the ball to a shooter, then charges at him as if to block the shot. After the shot, the passer/defender boxes out the shooter, then steps behind the three-point line himself. As the original shooter is tracking down his shot, the third player passes the ball to the new shooter, runs at him, and boxes him out after the shot. The first player to make 10 shots wins.

The "shoot and box" game teaches you to shoot with a little pressure.

5

REBOUNDING

44 NO REBOUNDS, NO RINGS

More rebounds means more shots,
which means more victories.

"No rebounds, no rings," says Miami Heat coach Pat Riley, who should know after winning four championships with the Los Angeles Lakers.

It doesn't take an NBA coach to know rebounding is important. Even a beginning youth league basketball player understands the logic: rebounding gets your team more shots, and if your team gets more shots than the opponent, you have a better chance of winning. This is especially true for younger players, who miss more shots.

National statistics confirm the importance of rebounding. The better rebounding team wins 80 percent of the time in high school.

Rebounding is the easiest basketball skill to learn. It's not about size or leaping ability—although those traits help. Rebounding is primarily about desire. Tony McAndrews, head coach of Division II Nova Southeastern University near Fort Lauderdale, says: "Height is overrated and heart is underrated." So if you're short, don't concede a single rebound to one of those trees in the paint. And if you're one of those giants, remember this: everyone else on the court is going after the ball, too. Thus, you should never take a rebound for granted.

Rebounding position is the precise position from which players can most effectively compete for a missed shot. But that position changes as the predicted shooter dribbles left or right, or passes the ball to a teammate on another part of the floor. That's why the best rebounders are the players who keep moving.

Rebounding requires heart and aggressiveness.

45 BOXING OUT

Make contact with your opponents to keep them off the boards.

To rebound, you want to get yourself to the place where you think a missed shot will go. And you want to be the only player in that position. To accomplish this, keep yourself between the basket and your opponent.

You can ensure this position while the shot is in the air: a 15-foot shot takes two seconds to reach the rim. You can do a lot in those two seconds.

The number-one thing to learn about boxing out is making contact with your opponent. When a shot goes up, reach out and touch him, preferably with your forearm to his chest and your rear end to his thighs, stopping all momentum toward the ball. (Coaches say "get a body on him," or "box out.") Younger players are reluctant to do this, maybe because they think it's a foul, or maybe they're just too timid.

Making contact stops your opponent's momentum to the ball. Stay lower than him so you'll have better leverage. Keep your knees bent, your hands up, and your arms at shoulder height.

When the ball comes your way, jump off both feet and grab the ball with both hands. Catch the ball and keep it under your chin, with your elbows wide. (This is called the *chin-it position*. Holding a rebound above your head or around your waist makes it too easy for the other players to slap it away.)

If it's an offensive rebound, try to put the ball back in the basket. If you're on defense, look to pass the ball to a teammate to start a fast break.

Don't rely on your teammates to get the rebound. Often guards will stand around watching a miss, waiting for the big men to retrieve the ball. Guards, too, must block out their opponent and then head toward the basketball.

Remember that more shots are missed than made. A player who assumes every shot taken will be missed, and who goes after each miss like the game depends on it, will often find the ball.

Make contact with your opponent, then jump up and grab the rebound.

46 TWO HANDS, TWO FEET

More rebounds will be yours if you jump off both feet and grab the ball with two hands.

Even baseball coaches know it: it's easier to catch a ball with two hands than with one. But did you know you can jump higher off two feet than off one?

When you think about it, it makes perfect sense. No matter what, your body weight is the same. But the amount of propulsion (OK, *hops*) is doubled when you have twice as much muscle providing the oomph.

The point of all this? You can gather many more rebounds if you jump off both feet and grab the ball with both hands.

When a shot goes up, bend your knees to jump quickly. Get your hands above your shoulders to catch any quick caroms. Again, you're assuming the shot will be missed, even if it's by your best shooter. If the ball actually goes in, you've lost nothing.

A good way for players, especially younger ones, to train their bodies for *two hands, two feet* is the wall bounce. Throw the ball off the wall and jump up like you're rebounding it. When the ball comes toward you, jump off both feet and tap the ball back toward the wall with both hands.

Try to tap the ball off the wall to yourself 10 times in a row. Make sure both of your feet are in the air each time (simulating rebounding). This exercise builds coordination, and for younger players is more manageable than tapping the ball off the backboard of a 10-foot hoop.

Remember to keep your feet at shoulder width for best balance. Also, while you're at the wall, get in a quick layup practice. Tap the ball off the wall with your right hand while jumping off your left foot. Go for 10 in a row. Then go left hand, right foot. This teaches your body the proper footwork for layups.

As young players grow, they will be able to graduate from wall bounces to rebounding the basketball off a regular hoop. If you have a portable hoop, lower the basket to eight feet or so. Parents can throw the ball off the basket and the player can practice grabbing the ball.

Again, emphasize jumping off both feet and catching the ball with both hands (going up strong). Of course, boxing out makes going up strong much easier.

If you grab the ball with both hands, it can't get knocked away.

47 PREDICT THE FLIGHT

Following the bouncing ball after a missed shot takes a little brain work. After awhile, it's no sweat.

What some refer to as a great rebounding instinct is really just logic. Much of rebounding is about knowing where a missed shot is likely to land. That *instinct* can be developed with careful study.

Shots from the corner are the easiest to gauge. Studies show that as many as 80 percent of all misses from one corner end up on the other side of the basket. If the shot is long, the ball has no other place to go. And if the shooter is barely short, the ball will catch the inside of the rim and kick farther away. Only a line drive from the corner that is decidedly short will carom back toward the shooter.

Some other tips for rebounding sleuths:

• Shots taken from the middle of the court usually return to the middle, unless the shooter is very wild. If a shot from, say, the top of the key misses either long or short, it will bounce back to the middle of the floor. And if it's left or right by just a little bit, it will catch the inside of the rim, probably hit the backboard, and fall near the basket.

• Common sense: longer shots often produce longer rebounds. They're put up there with more force, so they're more likely to produce a crazy bounce. (The advent of the three-pointer has brought about more rebounds like this.)

• Being in shape is the key to late-game rebounding. As the game goes on and players get tired, there is a greater likelihood of short and wild shots. That means if you keep running and moving, you're more apt to run down errant shots. This is especially true for offensive rebounds, where tired players often will forget to box you out.

Get in the position where you think a miss will land.

48 CHIN IT!

Put yourself in a position of strength after a defensive rebound.

After pushing out the nine other players on the floor to get a rebound, it's disheartening to have the ball poked away. The more quickly you can do something with the ball—pass, dribble, or shoot—the more off-balance your opponents will be. That's why you should move into the chin-it position after you pull down a rebound. It helps you protect the ball while also becoming an offensive threat.

Try to rebound the ball strong, with your feet slightly wider than your shoulders. Then it's more difficult for someone to knock you off-balance. Distribute your weight evenly between your heels and the balls of your feet. Keep your head and eyes up, looking for an outlet opening (dribble, pass, or shot). Place your hands on the side of the ball, and keep your forearms parallel to the floor and your elbows out. Hold the ball firmly on your chest, just slightly under your chin.

If a defensive player tries to slap the ball away from the side, he risks fouling you on the arm. If a player tries to tie you up for a jump ball, just pivot away, keeping your elbows wide. And on the rare occasions you get stripped from underneath, the ball will usually bounce off your chest or chin and you can retain possession. It's within the rules to pivot with your elbows wide, but you can't swing them back and forth like weapons. It's a violation, and a technical foul if you make contact with someone.

Once the ball is chinned, it's just a short maneuver into triple threat position:

• **Shoot:** A pump fake works especially well after an offensive rebound. The defense is already off-balance, having been beaten for the rebound, and the defenders are mentally discouraged. There's a good chance they'll swipe at the first hint of a shot.

- **Pass:** From the chin-it position, step toward your target and push your thumbs through the ball (more on the outlet pass later).

- **Dribble (right-handed):** Look to advance the ball somewhere: dribbling in place is a good way to get stripped and waste your good rebounding effort. In most cases, a dribble should be used to beat just one defender.

Chin-it works at all ages, for both boys and girls. The words are also a great verbal cue for teammates to use to remind each other after pulling down a rebound or gathering a loose ball in traffic.

Proper chin-it position: the elbows are wide and the stance is strong.

49 HIT THE OUTLET MAN

Take a fast-break opportunity and run with it.

The fast break is a beautiful thing. It means your team has moved downcourt quickly and worked the ball to an open player. The defense hasn't had time to set up. If you've been running on them a few times, your opponents are likely to start griping at each other.

It's a wonderful way to win. And most of the time, the fast break takes some contributions from the big men.

Fast breaks usually come in two forms: you've stolen the ball or you've rebounded one of the other team's misses. Let's deal with the latter.

You've successfully rebounded the ball and remembered to chin it. Now you're looking for a better ballhandler to get the ball down the court. Most of the time that guard will be near the sideline, away from the defense. That player is called the *outlet man*. He's away from the main action, just like an electrical outlet in a house is tucked off to the side of the room. Whichever side you rebound the ball on, look to your closest sideline. It's the guard's job to get there.

Then, it's either an overhead pass, a bounce pass, or a chest pass to the guard. (The baseball pass is dangerous because you have to pull your arm behind your head while you're presumably in traffic.) And guards, take note: it's your job to run toward the ball and meet the pass. A lot of balls are intercepted in the final step, while the offensive player is trying to get a running start downcourt.

A rebounder's job isn't finished once he lets go of the ball. You want to beat your defender down the floor. (Hey, after all, it is a fast break.) Choose a path nobody else, especially your point guard, is taking. Doing that makes the defense guard the whole floor.

Then sprint—don't jog!—down the court. If you do, and your defender doesn't, your guard will likely reward you with a pass for an easy shot.

The guards often will be at the foul line extended, waiting to get the ball to start a fast break.

50 OFFENSIVE REBOUNDING

Three maneuvers will help you get the missed shot before your opponent does.

The easiest way to get more shots for yourself? Rebound everyone else's misses.

Offensive rebounding is like all other rebounding, only magnified. The ball bounces most often toward those who want it the most. It's demoralizing to the other team, which has fought hard to make you miss, then failed to recover the ball. Not to mention that it prevents the fast break and can get the other team in foul trouble.

You'll get a lot more offensive rebounds if you don't allow yourself to be boxed out. Here are three maneuvers that will stop defenders from getting a body on you. They all take energy and a willingness to move your feet:

1. **Crossover step:** Fake the defender in one direction and go the other way. For example, if he moves too far to the right in response to your fake, quickly bring your right foot past his left leg and bump his body out of the way. A lot of good rebounders "sell" the fake by putting pressure on one side of the defender's back (the side they're not going toward). Many times you'll be boxed out from cutting to the middle of the floor. In those cases, dash toward the end line and then cut back inside your defender to get better position.

2. **Rear turn and roll:** This works best when the defender has done a pretty good job boxing you out. Place one foot between the defender's legs and execute a back pivot. Roll your rear end off his, spin off the defender, and keep your hands up, trying to establish inside position.

3. **Direct step:** If the defender hasn't gotten close enough to you to attempt a box out, dash right by him with a long, quick step.

When getting in position for a rebound, don't watch the flight of the ball. You can't change it anyway. Instead, think about what spot on the floor you want to be in, and keep your eyes on anything that's in the way.

Look to go back up with a shot after pulling down an offensive rebound.

51 HANDS UP!

Ways to build strength in your arms so they don't start to droop in the fourth quarter.

Players don't actually shrink as a basketball game progresses, but it may seem that way under the boards. Many rebounds that are pulled down near the rim in the first quarter can nearly hit the floor before finding a willing hand late in the game.

That's because as the fourth quarter approaches, players are less likely to extend themselves fully to grab a rebound. And if they do reach all the way for a ball, their arms are often tired and vulnerable to having the ball poked away.

As vital as the legs are to basketball, we tend to forget about arm conditioning. Many rebounds are lost simply because players don't have their hands even up near their shoulders, let alone fully extended with the elbows up by the ears (what some coaches call the *work position*).

Here are three conditioning exercises that will help you pull down those late-game caroms:

1. **Wall dribbling:** Stand only four or five inches away from the wall. Pitty-pat the ball with your fingertips while jumping, keeping your arms in the work position. Do them in sets of 20. When your arms feel weak, keep going; you want to condition yourself to get your arms up *especially* when you're tired.

2. **Continuous jumping:** Hop off two feet with your arms above your head. Try to go for three minutes. If you're practicing with a friend, try to keep talking while jumping. (Conditioning note: conversation during a workout can increase cardiovascular conditioning by as much as 50 percent.) Play music to keep your mind active. This is also great to do toward the end of team practice because it replaces running line drills, yet teaches a basketball-related skill.

3. **Over-the-top-tipping:** With a partner on the other side of the basket, tip the ball with two hands back and forth to each other. Your arms must constantly be in the work position, even when the ball is on the other side of the basket.

Remember to build up your hands and fingers, too. They are the key to holding on to the ball. Fingertip pushups, typewriter dribbles, and squeezing a rubber ball will help. Better yet, get an old basketball, let just a little bit of the air out, and practice palming it. And when you're weightlifting, remember to do those arm curls.

Build up arm strength and endurance with the over-the-top tipping drill.

52 FREE-THROW REBOUNDS

There are offensive and defensive strategies competing at the foul line for the missed shot.

The lower the level of basketball, the more opportunity for offensive rebounds of missed free throws. That's because in some leagues, 50 percent is considered good foul shooting.

A little bit of gamesmanship can overcome the position advantage the defenders have. They line up on the two inside spots, so all they have left is the easy job of blocking out.

You can make *easy* a relative term. When a free-throw shooter lets go of the ball, begin stepping over the defender's foot closest to you. When the ball hits the rim, put your foot down and push the opponent out of position with your rear end.

If you can't grab the ball, go for the back tap. The defense ordinarily places four players on the line for a free throw, so if you can tap the ball past the foul line, your team's odds of getting the ball are good. And with the three-pointer, the offense often will get a wide-open look.

On defense, not getting the rebound can be a back-breaker. So put all five defenders in the lane: most teams will put four defenders in and have the fifth head downcourt. This rarely pays off in a fast break; it's better to go ahead and put all your players to use in the lane so the defense can do one of these three things:

1. **Squeeze the best rebounder:** Use your player with inside position and the player in the third position to do nothing but block out the opponent who can hurt you the most.

2. **Block out the crashing guards:** Sometimes players will dash in from the three-point line. They're easy to block out if you have teammates in the lane.

3. **Box out the shooter:** Foul shots missed short will bounce right back. Good teams will call out "I have the shooter" among themselves before the ball is even handed to the foul shooter. That way everyone can determine what his job is.

Also use the dead-ball time during a free throw to quietly communicate with your teammates. If their best player has three fouls and you want to attack him, remind your teammates. Encourage those whose heads are hanging, and settle down those who are upset about some earlier play that they can't change.

A lot of times teams will fall asleep at the foul line. The defense might still be upset about the call, or may be passive because they don't want another quick foul. This is when being the most alert will pay off.

To beat a block-out, slip your leg over the defender's leg.

6

DEFENSE

53 USE YOUR HEAD

Defense isn't rocket science, but it takes brain power and a willingness to study your opponent to score high with coaches.

Defense is as much a mental game as a physical one. If you play it well, there will almost always be a uniform for you.

To play defense well takes a lot of self-discipline and determination. Those are traits anyone can develop, whether quick or slow, tall or short.

"My man won't score, and my man won't get a rebound," should be your attitude. Remember, each time you stop somebody from scoring affects the scoreboard the same as if you scored a basket yourself.

Here is where playground play comes in handy. Once teams are chosen, pick out the *best* player on the other team. Make it your personal goal to stop him. Apply the fundamentals outlined in the next few pages (stance, forcing to the weak hand, shuffle steps, and denying passes) and watch him get frustrated. You'll be surprised how often you can defend someone who's bigger, faster, or stronger than you just by using your smarts.

Here are some questions you can ask as you study your opponent:

- What and where are his favorite shots?

- Is he right- or left-handed? Can he use his weak hand?

- What is his favorite move?

- Is he a good dribbler or a bad dribbler?

- Is he a good shooter or a bad shooter?

- Does he cut to the basket a lot?

- Does he do well in the low post?

- Will we need to double-team him?

Why should you buy into playing defense to the best of your abilities? Think about it: there's only one ball, but two teams. That means you're spending 50 percent of a game on offense and the other 50 percent playing defense.

And to win, you must get the job done at both ends of the court.

Know which players need double-teaming and react quickly to guard them.

54 DEFENSIVE STANCE

To prevent easy baskets, put your body
in the best position to react.

A boxer. A shortstop. A tennis player. A defensive stopper. All four must begin with what sports announcers call *good athletic position*. Your knees are bent so there's tension in the thighs. You're on your toes. One foot is slightly ahead of the other. You're ready to react in any of the four directions: left, right, forward, or backward.

Basketball coaches call it the *defensive stance*. It's mostly common sense: you can defend better if your body is in position to react. If you want to move from a standing-up position, your first motion is to bend your knees. Why not get a head start?

The idea of defense should be to prevent easy baskets. Once you get containment, then concentrate on pressuring and stealing the ball.

Playing defense with your feet means that you don't reach in and try to steal the ball. Reaching in is a lazy way to play and often results in a foul. You're putting yourself off-balance and forcing your teammates to leave their players to cover yours. Instead, stay in your stance and concentrate on containing your man. Keep your knees bent and your legs about shoulder-width apart. Your arms are partially raised where you can grab the ball if your man fumbles it.

Early in the year, my team spends 10 minutes a day practicing getting into a defensive stance. It sounds overly simplistic, but it helps drill into players the difference between just standing on defense and getting ready to compete. Just the word *stance* has effectively been used as a verbal cue during games for a player who doesn't look ready to play defense.

And when it comes to competing, tell players this: "No stance? No chance."

When defending a player with the ball, keep your knees bent and hands out.

55 LEFT FOOT FORWARD

*Apply pressure to take away the
opponent's strong dribbling hand.*

A good defender dictates to the offense what to do. You'll want to take away your opponent's strongest dribbling hand (usually the right).

Start with your left foot forward so you can force him to the left. When he dribbles in that direction, move your feet and get to a spot in front of him that will make him change direction. Keep your head lower than the offensive player's, usually level with his chest.

Once he picks up his dribble, close in aggressively. Trace the ball with your hands. The more pressure you put on the ball, the harder it is for an offensive player to pass to an open teammate. (Think of a quarterback trying to throw the ball against a ferocious pass rush.)

How close should you be to your man? It depends on the situation.

If he's out at midcourt and a good ballhandler, give him a full step or two. Your goal is containment; if he gets around you, his team has five players attacking your four. Generally, the closer he is to the basket with the ball, the closer you are to him.

In a one-on-one situation out on the wing, you're close enough to bother a jump shot but not close enough to block it. If you are that close, he'll likely be able to drive around you. If he's made two or three shots from outside during the game and you have a big man behind you to help, you should play closer, about a foot away, forcing him to put the ball on the floor.

Again, good defense is about dictating to the opponent. If you have a good stance and a good brain, you'll be able to take away the offensive player's strength.

Force dribblers to use the weak hand by keeping your left foot forward.

56 SHUFFLE STEP

A footwork technique to make you as quick as you can be.

We're all different. Some of us are quick, and some are not. To guard your man effectively, you must get the most out of whatever amount of quickness you do have. Learning to shuffle step well helps make you as quick as you can be. It's a way to keep with a defender without merely running alongside him or "hugging" him.

The best way to work on your shuffle step technique is to do it in super-slow motion. That way you worry only about form and body positioning. It doesn't take long to train yourself how to shuffle step.

Bend your knees and stand on the balls of your feet. Your hands should be open and your arms extended to your sides. Because your left foot is forward (*stance!*), let's presume you're forcing your opponent to his left. Take a quick half-step with your left foot, then a regular step with your right. This gets your momentum going in that direction. Then it's full steps...left, right, left, right. Your heels never touch the ground—if they do, you're off-balance—and your feet never get closer than a foot apart, for the same reason.

As you shuffle step, still in slow motion, visualize a dribbler going to the left side of the floor. You want to be ahead of the ballhandler by a half-step, so if he turned to go toward the basket, you would be taking a charge.

Eventually the ballhandler will reverse directions. No problem. Pivot off your back foot, turn your front hip quickly, and you're in position to shuffle in the opposite direction. Try that in slow motion, too.

Lots of teams practice the shuffle step by zigzagging up and down the floor, sometimes with a dribbler to defend. If you do this, concentrate on technique first. It's not a race. This is a case where putting time in now on stance and footwork will pay off later.

Small, quick steps can make you harder to get around.

57 HELPING YOUR TEAMMATES

A talking defense turns one-on-one situations into one-on-five.

If you knew a tall shot-blocking teammate was behind you on defense, you would guard your man tightly and be more apt to try to steal the ball. And if you knew a teammate to your right could help create a double-team, you would more than likely force your man that way.

How do you know these things in a game? Simple. Your teammates tell you.

Never on a basketball court is talking as important as when playing defense. Go to your local small college game and sit near the floor. Sure, watch how they play defense. But just as important, listen.

"You have help to your right!"

"Screen left!"

"There's help behind you!"

What the defense is doing is turning a one-on-one situation into a one-on-five! When a dribbler does beat somebody, the closest teammate has to get over in front of the driver to prevent a layup. The most efficient way to help is for everyone to know ahead of time what the plan is.

If your player is *one pass away*, meaning the player with the ball could pass to your man for a chance to score, you should be one-third of the way toward helping. (So if the dribbler is at the point and your man is at the wing, 30 feet away, you can cheat 10 feet toward the ball.) That position gives you a chance of helping, and gives you plenty of time to run over and defend your man if the ball is passed to him.

If your player is *two passes away*, meaning the person with the ball can't immediately pass it to him, you can get over and help much more. Play halfway between your man and the dribbler. For example, if the one with the ball is on the left wing and your man is in the right corner, you should be directly in front of the basket. You have plenty of time to help against the drive, and plenty of time to recover and guard your man.

Team defense is a series of minor adjustments, so each time the ball is passed you should be moving either toward the ball or toward your man. The fact that you're always in motion is just a bonus; you'll see more loose balls and errant passes end up in your hands.

If everyone on your team helps each other, you'll see more victories.

If the player with the ball has a live dribble, you need to help your teammate in case of a drive.

58 GUARDING WITHOUT THE BALL

Anticipate where your man is going and get a head start.

Five players to defend. One ball. The math is easy: you're going to spend four times as much of your defense against someone trying to get ready to get the ball than you will on the player actually trying to score.

So that means you can just rest, right?

Of course not. Instead, use the Boy Scout motto: be prepared.

If your opponent is any kind of a player at all, you know he is thinking about getting into a good spot to catch a pass for a favorite shot. You should be trying to read his mind.

He needs two things to score: good position and the ball. You'll need to keep your eye on both.

The ball part is easy, especially if your teammate hollers out "I got the man with the ball!" Think of defending his cuts to open spots as a series of foot races between you and him.

Know how to win every race? Easy. Get a head start. For example if the ball is over on the right wing and he wants to cut from the left wing into the middle, go ahead and get one-third of the way there. (Remember *one pass away* from Tip 57.) Use your body as a deterrent. Keep the hand closest to the ball outstretched and keep the foot closest to the ball in the path an imaginary pass would go. Coaches call this keeping your *ball-side hand* and *ball-side foot* in the *passing lane*.

Again, the most important thing is to get away from your man a little bit, and stay ahead of where he will cut. Coaches yell out "Stop hugging your man!" from the bench as a reminder for defenders to cheat toward the ball.

The added benefit from *getting a head start* is that you're in position to help if a teammate gets beaten off the dribble.

Sometimes your man will have more than one spot open to cut to. Unless you read minds, you can't really tell where he's going, so defend the spot with the better shot. And if they're both good shots, you'll have to rely on team- mates to help you out—which is *another* reason why talking on defense is so important.

How do you win a race to an open spot?
Get a head start.

59 DEFENDING THE INSIDE PLAYER

Playing good defense doesn't mean just shot-blocking. Establish your position so your man doesn't even get the ball.

He can't score if he doesn't get the ball.

That's the attitude to take when defending big men under the basket.

If you think inside defense is all about shot-blocking, you're starting to defend too late. It's about position. A couple of guidelines:

• **If the inside man is much taller than you:** You'll have to play partially in front of him. You have to figure once he catches the ball, he'll have an easy score. So make it as difficult as possible for passers, and rely on teammates to cover any lob passes over your head. They'll need to talk to you about where they're helping from. (Notice a pattern here yet?)

• **If the inside man is much shorter than you:** You can play behind him most of the time. If you're 6 feet and your man is 5-foot-6, you'll be able to get by on harassing the shooter and shot-blocking.

More technique is required when you and your man are about the same height. When the ball is anywhere but in the corner, you'll play three-quarters in front of your man, and use some techniques from Tip #58, Guarding Without the Ball. The ball-side hand and ball-side foot are outstretched to deter any passes. Your other arm can rest on his hip, but don't wrap your arm around his waist—restricting movement that much is a foul.

If an offensive player in the corner gets the ball, you have to hustle around to the baseline side and prevent a quick pass from the corner for an easy layup. The taller/shorter rules apply here: go behind him if you can stop his shot, in front to deny the ball the whole time if you think you can't.

Play three-quarters of the way around your man so the pass can't come inside easily.

60 SHOT-BLOCKING

***Get good rebound position instead of going for the block.
But when you do block, deflect the ball to keep it in play.***

It's the play of last resort.

If you're trying to block a shot, that means the offense has maneuvered its way into scoring position and feels confident enough to attempt to score. Nevertheless, a blocked shot can be a beautiful basketball play to watch—when it's done right.

In a one-on-one situation, the percentages favor defensive position, harassing the shooter, and concentrating on establishing rebounding position, rather than going for the block. (Think about drawing charges, not blocking shots.)

Most blocks come when big men help out their guards and forwards. The percentages in favor of a block when a tall defender comes over to knock away a shot from a shorter opponent are a lot better than when he tries to swat someone his own size. A good shot-blocker merely deflects the ball, keeping it in play to start a fast break.

Think about the angles: it is easier to reach to the right side of a player with your left hand, instead of torquing your body to get to the ball with your strong hand. (Maybe this explains why a lot of great shot-blockers, such as David Robinson and Bill Russell, are left-handed.) The defender's hand goes straight up, so the shooter is putting the ball into his hand. Bringing your arm down to meet the ball often brings about a hack—and a seat on the bench because of foul trouble.

Keep your feet on the floor. Being a leaper makes you vulnerable to being faked out. Former Boston Celtics great Bill Russell said: "The idea is not to block every shot. The idea is to make your opponent believe you might block every shot."

Once you've blocked one shot, it gets the opponents thinking. That's to your advantage. Even if you know you can't block a shot, run at the shooter with your hand up. If they start missing short, a lot of times it's because your presence forced them to rush their shots, bringing their arms down too quickly.

For competitive reasons, let your actions be what gets into their head, not your mouth. When some opponent blocks a shot and bellows something like "Not in my house!" it only serves as motivation.

Tell players when they block a shot to act like they've done it before. All the woofing and celebrating just points to the fact that it must have been a special occasion for you to have made a good play.

Use your right hand to block a left-handed shooter; use your left hand to block a righty.

FOOTWORK

7

61 THE FOUNDATION OF YOUR GAME

Making the right move depends on how quickly you think on your feet.

Your footwork can gain you a step—or lose you one. It can get you the proper angle to make a cut or a shot, or it can put you in no-man's land.

You handle the ball an average of 10 percent of the time (10 players sharing one basketball), but you need to be working for good position to defend, cut, or shoot 100 percent of the time. That's why players need to develop excellent footwork.

Fortunately, through practice and repetition, footwork can become second nature. Practice some of the exercises on the next pages. Use the baseline, three-point line, and lane lines to help you get a feel for positioning your body on the basketball court.

Go at walk-through speed at first, but keep practicing until your moves are habitual. You'll need that confidence for game time, when you're worrying about making your moves against a defense. Any move not applicable at game speed won't be usable.

What's the goal of footwork? Getting your body in the best possible place on the basketball court—and then being able to make a move from there. If you don't have a good base for your shot—feet at shoulder width and hips low—it's difficult to shoot it consistently. And that means lower shooting percentages and bad habits. If a player is standing straight up, with his hands on his hips, he is not ready to make that split-second move.

That's why a lot of coaches advocate jumping rope. The routines of left-foot, right-foot, both-feet require balance and coordination needed to quickly get in position.

Correct positioning is the foundation of your entire game. It's how players who aren't fast runners survive against those who are.

Jumping rope helps develop balance and coordination.

62 JUMP STOP

Learning to brake correctly will keep your offense going in the right direction.

If a ballhandler and his defender are equally quick, what advantage does the offense have? Offensive players know where they're going—and they know when they're going to stop.

Face it, you're going to stop sometime—that's the idea. The important part is stopping under control. That is where the jump stop, or quick stop, comes in.

Just as getting a quick start is important in basketball, it is equally important to be able to come to a quick stop where you can make a play.

If you are off-balance when you stop, you then have to take the time to set yourself up. This wastes time, even if only for a second. This is about all it takes for the defensive player to regain any advantage you had over him.

Stop off the run by landing with both feet on the floor at the same time. The heels touch first and your toes act as brakes to slow you down. Your knees are flexed, back bent slightly backward. This eliminates your forward movement. By crouching as you land, you are now in the *fundamental basketball position.* You are ready to shoot, receive a pass, or cut in another direction.

If you need to change or reverse direction, use the stride stop. It's also the best way to get your body prepared to shoot a jump shot off the dribble. To make a stride stop, land on your rear foot and then on your front foot. The rear foot becomes the pivot foot, so don't move it if you stop dribbling. Keep your knees flexed and your back tilted slightly backward to slow your forward momentum.

I love the jump stop on layups because going off two feet gives players more control. It also helps them go up strong to the basket, negating any bumps and nudges they'll receive along the way.

It's also critical for guards in a fast break to make a good two-footed stop before passing the ball. They have better control that way, and their momentum won't carry them out of the play.

The jump stop helps you stop under control.

63 JAB STEP

Get the defense to react, then make your move.

To keep a defender at bay, borrow some strategy from boxers. The boxer on the attack will often use the jab to throw his opponent off-balance. If the jab is done well, the attacking boxer will follow with a bigger move.

The same is true for the skilled basketball player. He uses the jab step to set up his defender, then goes for the kill.

For a right-handed player in triple threat position, the right foot is slightly forward. A jab is a step with the right (non-pivot) foot and a quick return to a balanced triple threat. The defender will tend to back off, which gets his weight going backward, off-balance.

Use that time to size up the situation. If you've kept your balance, the jump shot is open. And if the defender reacts too quickly, he'll sell out his balance to try to defend the shot. (So fake the shot and you're past him like a bull rumbling past a matador.)

A related move is the rocker step. Instead of taking a step forward, you drop your right foot behind you. The defender will often become too confident and lunge for the ball. If he does, then it's very effective to sweep the ball past your body (see Tip 6 on the sweep, page 14) and drive past him with a hard left-hand dribble.

After you've mastered the jab and the rocker, the mind games really begin. A halfhearted jab or rocker can get the defender thinking, and an all-out fake to the other side will totally cross him up. There aren't many young players who double-fake well, so if you can do it, you'll be leaving your defenders looking silly.

And your team will win by a knockout.

Use the jab to get the defender to react. If he lunges toward you, drive toward the basket.

64 V-CUT/L-CUT

Sharpen these two steps to slash opponents out of the way.

Know where you're going. That's the advantage of being on offense.

The V-cut and the L-cut are the two most popular ways to beat a defender. Both can be related to football: the V-cut is a fake followed by a sprint past the defense; the L-cut is like a square-in or square-out pattern.

Practice making both cuts by having a chair act as the defender. A passer from the wing can deliver you the ball. You'll be honing three skills at once if you concentrate on cutting, catching, and making the layup. And whoever is passing you the ball can work on throwing overhead or sideways bounce passes because those are the two most common ways to throw the ball into the lane against a defense.

As in football, if you cut halfheartedly, you won't get open. Rounding off a cut, rather than going at a sharp angle, is basically a wasted move. The defense can react easily and you won't be open enough to receive the ball from your teammates.

- **V-cut:** Think *fake and break*. If the ball is at the wing and you're at the point, act like you're running to the opposite wing. Once you have placed all your weight on the front foot, the one farthest from the ball, quickly push off that foot and make a quick change of direction. Stick your hand up in the air to give the passer a target. The V-cut is also effective for wing players who are having trouble getting open. Simply fake in the direction you want your opponent to go, then run in the direction that you want to go.

- **L-cut:** The L-cut, also called the square-off cut, works because it's such a sharp change in direction. It works best when you break toward the ball, fake the defender one way, then push off in the opposite direction. Use a head nod or a target receiving hand to tip off the passer which way you really want to go.

As soon as you catch a pass after cutting, your main objective is to get your shoulders square to the basket and have your feet shoulder-width apart. You've worked this hard to get the ball: now do something with it.

The V-cut: head in one direction, push hard off your front foot, and change direction.

65 DROP STEP

After you go up for the ball, know which way to turn.

When you have your back to the basket, the drop step is the simplest way to get past your defender and to the hoop. The drop step paves the way to rotate your body and go strong to the basket.

First, feel where the defense is. You want to pin your opponent behind you by using good footwork, positioning yourself in line with your prospective passer.

If you catch the ball by the painted block on the right side of the floor, you can beat the opponent to your left for a layup. With your right foot as the pivot, step toward the basket with your left foot, turning your toes 90 degrees so they are in line with the backboard.

As you turn, dribble the ball low and hard once with your right hand. Turn the rest of your body toward the backboard as the ball bounces and pick up your dribble, using the jump stop.

You'll be at a 45-degree angle to the hoop, shoulders square to the backboard, with the defender on your left hip, sealed away from the ball.

The key is turning your foot. Once you get the lower part of your leg past your defender and facing the basket, the rest of your body will naturally rotate to the hoop. When you practice your drop steps, exaggerate the foot turn so it comes easily in games.

Catching a pass in the post while midair makes the drop step twice as lethal. When you jump to catch a pass and land on both feet at the same time, either foot can be your pivot foot. Now, don't move: you'll give away your advantage.

The idea of using the drop step to score is the same from the left side, except the left foot is the pivot foot and you step toward the basket with your right.

What makes you the most unpredictable is having the drop step to the middle of the floor in your arsenal, too. From the right side, drop your right foot, then make a quick left-hand dribble and left-hand layup. You'll find that you won't really have to leap that much because your body positioning has made it difficult for the defender to get to the ball.

Step past the defender and use your leg to seal him off from your path.

66 AGILITY JUMP

Not quick enough?
Here are some ways to get faster and stronger.

Agile players can pivot and jump—and do it quickly. Certain exercises can improve your agility, but you'll need a little equipment.

Take two boxes (like what grocery stores ship fruit in) and a 6- to 10-foot broomstick. A rake handle or anything like it will do. Put the boxes 6 to 8 feet apart and put the stick on top of the boxes. Ideally, you'll want the boxes 12 to 15 inches high.

Starting with your toes parallel to the extended stick, jump over the stick and immediately jump back to the other side. Make sure you're jumping off both feet, from side to side. Try to do 20 in a row without taking any extra steps.

Now work on alternating jumping with pivoting. Change positions so your feet and body are facing the stick. Spring up and over the stick, landing on the balls of your feet. Pivot 180 degrees to your left and jump straight over the stick again, then right pivot back into starting position.

As you continue to progress, raise the boxes higher.

Another way to increase your agility is to make practices harder on yourself than on anyone else. There are a variety of props to help you:

• **Weight jackets:** Sporting goods stores sell vest-like jackets that can be buckled at your navel. Small lead weights are placed in the pockets, which are evenly distributed throughout your upper body. These jackets make you top-heavy, so keeping your balance and footwork precise is essential.

• **Strength shoes:** If you're a size 10, wearing these shoes is like wearing a size 14. Because they're heavy, it's difficult to pick up your feet. The great part is playing once they come off!

• **Galoshes:** Old-fashioned rain boots can slide over your tennis shoes and help you build leg strength. Practice the agility jump series in this tip or practice defensive slides while wearing the galoshes. You'll know what it's like to be in the fourth quarter of a rugged game.

Pretend you're a pogo stick.

67 MARK EATON DRILL

This NBA player got better when he jumped around where X marked the spot.

Five small dots didn't get Mark Eaton from auto mechanic to the NBA All-Star Game—but they sure helped. Eaton, who played for the Utah Jazz from 1982–1993, led the NBA in blocked shots, averaging more than 3.5 blocks per game. At one point in his life, Eaton was the world's tallest auto mechanic. The 7-foot-4 giant worked in California fixing cars; his size alone wasn't enough to make him a basketball player.

After shuffling through junior college and two years at UCLA, Eaton joined the Utah Jazz. His coach, Frank Layden, realized Eaton would never have the grace and foot speed of a Michael Jordan or even a David Robinson. But if Eaton could just improve his footwork a fraction, his height would make him a functional NBA player. He told Eaton they would work together for one year to improve his agility.

"It's funny that people would use me as an example for footwork, because mine wasn't very good," Eaton says. "But there's no doubt that by working on maintaining balance and increasing quickness that I was able to play in the NBA."

He used a complicated routine mixing left-, right-, and two-footed hops. Here is a simpler version of what he did.

Using athletic tape, make a big X out of the five dots. Put each of the four surrounding pieces about one foot away from the center piece. (If you don't have tape, make marks with a piece of chalk.)

The idea of this drill is to hop quickly from one dot to another using your left foot, right foot, or both, like a big man has to do during a game.

Start in the middle and hop off your right foot to the upper right dot, then back to the center. Then hop back and forth to the three other surrounding dots (still with the right foot), always returning to the middle. Do the same routine with the left foot, then go through the jumps using both feet.

Now it gets tricky. Spin halfway around (180 degrees) on each hop. So your first hop, to the upper right, has you facing the middle dot. The hop returning to the middle dot has you facing forward again. Again, do this series with your right foot only, left foot only, and with both feet, making the half-turn while in the air. Concentrate on keeping your hips low when you land and your weight evenly distributed.

Try to complete all six sets of jumps without stopping. Working under the boards will seem easy by comparison.

Hop from one spot to another
to improve agility.

68 PIVOT OFF THE INSIDE FOOT

Turn, turn, turn—knowing the correct way puts you closer to the basket.

An 8-foot shot is obviously easier than a 12-footer. You can get the closer shot just by pivoting off your inside foot.

As you make a cut to the basket, remember to catch the ball while you're in the air, landing on both feet. That way you can pivot off either foot. Then it's common sense: pivot off the foot closer to the basket.

This is especially useful when cutting from one wing into the middle of the lane. If you're coming from the right side, a right-foot pivot is more efficient.

Use the lines in the key area to help gauge how your pivot is helping you. If you catch the ball at the foul line, try to pivot inside the lane. If you catch the ball at the top of the key, try to pivot inside the circle. This also gets you in the habit of attacking the basket, and the defenders eventually will dread you and back off.

Cement your pivoting habits and work on your shooting at the same time by using a three-man elbow shooting drill. Put a chair at the end of each side of the foul line. Start at one elbow, take the ball out of the chair, pivot with the foot closer to the basket, and shoot. Then run to the other elbow, pivot with the other foot, and shoot. Meanwhile, one of the other players serves as the rebounder, passing the ball to the third person, who places the balls in the chairs for you. See who can make the most shots in one minute.

You can get closer to the basket by using your shoulders, too. If you're dribbling toward the hoop, roll your inside shoulder down by your belt buckle. That makes it look like you're driving to the basket, and the defender will back off, respecting the drive.

Take the ball from each chair at the elbow and pivot toward the basket.

69 THE STEP-THROUGH

A change of direction throws defenders off-guard.

After you've learned the simple pivot and shoot and can drop-step well, practice the step-through. It's a change-of-direction move that works especially well when defenders lock their knees or prematurely leap in anticipation of a shot. It's a bit complicated, but it's the way to counter the shot-blockers who are expecting you to simply turn and shoot.

Use these methods to turn the step-through into a layup:

• Catch the ball on the right painted block and left-foot pivot toward the baseline, acting like you are about to shoot a normal right-handed turnaround jump shot away from the defense. But instead of shooting, do a head fake and quickly sweep the ball from your right shoulder to your left knee. Then quickly step with your right foot outside of the defender's right foot and into the center of the lane. Take one quick, low bounce and lay the ball in left-handed.

Turn into the middle, fake a shot, and quickly pull the ball to the other side, then quickly step past the defense.

• The other move from the right gets you a layup toward the baseline. Right-foot pivot into the lane, faking a jump shot from your left shoulder. Quickly sweep the ball to your right knee. This time, put your left foot outside the defender's and take a quick right-handed dribble for the layup.

• From the left block, right-foot pivot to the outside of the lane to get a quick sweep into the lane for a right-handed layup.

And use a left-foot pivot into the lane for a quick sweep toward the baseline for a left-handed layup. Each time, remember to get your foot outside the defender's, like a forward version of the drop step.

The step-through is a move to practice at half speed until you get the footwork down. But it has to be at full speed against the defense, or it's simply a wasted motion. It's especially true on the sweep: if you have the ball within the defender's reach too long, it can get poked away.

THE BIG
MAN'S GAME

70 BIG HEART MAKES A BIG MAN

Playing under the basket will test your ticker.

Height is overrated. Footwork is underrated. And heart, as usual, is the great determinant. Keep that in mind while learning all facets of basketball, but especially post play. If all factors are equal, it helps to be tall—but all factors aren't equal.

Stay big, not tall should be your rule in the post. When you have your back to the basket, you're expecting a pass from the outside. To keep your defender from intercepting that pass, you'll want to make yourself big.

Bend your knees so you feel a little tightness in your thighs. Take a wider-than-normal stance. This gives you a low center of gravity. Keep your hands up and your elbows out; this keeps the defender farther from the ball.

The move you use depends on the defense. If they're up close, you can spin around them for a layup. If they're sagging off, you should pivot and face the basket; from there it's either a shot or a quick drive.

Once you catch the ball near the basket, you need to score. Developing your skills near the basket will help you. Review the shooting chapter (Chapter 4), paying special attention to layups and the Mikan drill.

If you want more, try the tip drill: Jumping off your left foot, tip the ball off the backboard 5 times with your right hand. Then tip 5 with your left hand while jumping off your right foot (just like a layup). Then tip 5 with both hands, jumping off both feet. Work your way up to 10 tips of each (30 total).

When game time comes around, contact is inevitable under the basket. This is where heart comes in. Learn to enjoy contact; in most cases it helps you figure out where the defense is.

Unless you play a very poor team, most of your shots will be challenged. You'll be nudged, pushed, even hacked. And if you're not careful, the defense will take your mind off the number-one goal: getting the ball into the basket.

Don't let them do it.

Sometimes play in the paint requires battling for the ball.

71 GETTING OPEN INSIDE

Post players are the centers of attention.

It's one thing for your coach and teammates to want to get the ball inside to you, the big man. It's altogether another to do it successfully.

Face it: if you're taller than anyone else, it's pretty difficult to disguise it. Not only will your defender be doing his best to "play big," but his teammates are all ready to help at even the hint of a pass to you near the basket.

The post man is the focal point of the offense (no, that doesn't always mean the most prolific shooter). When the ball goes inside the paint, the guards get more time for outside shots even if the defense just *leans* toward the lane.

Before the ball even comes close to coming in, you're playing a mind game. And you had better win. Here are some tips for getting open inside:

• **Timing:** It is useless to have good position inside, when your point guard is still at midcourt. Most of the time you'll have a two-second window of excellent position; after that, the defense recovers. By keeping eye contact with your guards, you'll know when the right time to pass and receive is.

• **Direct traffic:** When you know you can get a good shot if you get the pass from the corner, point to your guard to throw the ball to a teammate standing in the corner. When you know you're not open, wave the passer off—they'll throw the ball to a teammate who will try to get it to you from another angle. Note: rarely can a pass to the big man come from the top of the key. There are just too many ways for the defense to help.

• **Give yourself room:** If you're caught too far under the basket, you run out of choices. It's better to catch the ball above the square along the foul line than below it. That way it's still possible to shoot the ball off the backboard or to reverse it to the other side of the floor.

Direct traffic, telling the guards where to pass the ball.

72 CATCHING THE BALL

The guards are like pitchers, your hand like a baseball mitt.

The coach wants the ball passed in to you, the post player. The guards are trying their best to do it. Here's how you help:

Make sure you give the passer a good target. Your hand farthest from the defender should be like a catcher's mitt; stick it up there and invite the pass. Sticking your arm up in the air is a cue to the passer to throw the ball.

Keep your other elbow at least shoulder height to ward off invading defenders. Hold your ground, but don't push off: that would be an offensive foul.

When the ball comes, look the ball into your hands. Use both hands if at all possible. Catching the pass is the most important task at that moment. Everything else can wait.

A lot of people advocate jumping to the ball. By catching the ball in the air and landing on both feet simultaneously, you can use either foot for pivoting. That doubles your options against a defender.

Although you are encouraging the passer to get you the ball to the hand farthest from the defense, concentrate on using two hands. This gives you greater control and more options.

Practice catching bad passes, too. In practice, have the guards throw some balls at your feet and well above your head. By practicing getting to those kinds of balls, you'll realize that your range is much greater than you thought. Plus, it will cement the fundamentals you're practicing.

Once you've caught the ball, pull it right under your chin, just as in the chin-it position used for rebounding. Your elbows are wide and your balance is low. In a second or two you'll be making a basket. Don't forget to thank your passers while you run back on defense.

Catching the ball in the air sets you up to pivot off either foot.

73 TENNIS BALL DRILL

Learn to catch a small ball—and raise a racket.

Most basketball skills can be improved with practice, and catching the ball is no exception. To quickly improve your hands, think small. Use tennis balls.

You'll need a patient passer to help you. Stand about 12 feet from him and assume the normal big man's position: bend your knees in a wider-than-normal stance for a low center of gravity. Keep your hands up and your elbows out.

Have the passer throw you a tennis ball. Because it's so small, you'll learn to keep your palms facing the passer. If the palms face each other, then you're grabbing, not catching, and the ball will slip through.

At first, have the passer throw the ball with a little arc to it so you can handle it. When you get better, ask for line drives. You have less time to gauge the throw and must react solely on technique.

When you've learned to catch the ball well with your palms facing out, learn to catch the tennis ball in the air. Jump off two feet and land on two. Pull the pass down into the chin-it position, just as if you were posting up in a game.

Once you've mastered that—and don't be upset if it takes some time—start with your back to the passer. Have him yell "turn" once the pass is released. After executing a left or right pivot, you'll have less time to gauge the flight of the ball, and it'll be tougher on you— which is the whole idea behind getting better.

Catch the ball with your palms facing out.

74 THE PICK AND ROLL

Force the defenders into making decisions.
The more decisions they make, the greater your
chances to capitalize on their errors.

It's the oldest play in basketball, but defenders still can't stop it. It helped John Stockton and Karl Malone of the Utah Jazz into the NBA Finals twice, and will eventually get them into the basketball Hall of Fame.

If the pick and roll can drive the world's best defensive teams in the NBA crazy, imagine what it could do to your next opponent.

At the very least, the pick and roll forces the defense to make decisions, and the more decisions a defense has to make, the greater the chances for error. And the upside goes much higher: bad switches by the defense can result in layups for your big man or guard, not to mention open jump shots.

The pick and roll is most effective when there are no other defenders on your side of the floor. That's why it's nice to take the ball to one side of the floor—where three of the five defenders will likely go—and then reverse it quickly to the other side, against two players.

The play is especially effective if your team has a left-handed player to reverse the ball to on that side of the court. Think about it: the defensive players have all properly gone over to help on the right (ball) side of the floor. And their inclination, if they're well-schooled, is to try to force their opponents to the left. Even though they know a player is left-handed, it takes them a split-second to adjust.

It's best to first practice the pick and roll using a chair or just one person as the defense. That helps get the footwork down, which—as in all of basketball—is the key.

At first, it's best to practice the pick and roll against just one person.

75 SCREENS

Make contact with the defense, and hold it for a second.

Good screens involve contact. They're not for the faint of heart. That doesn't mean you're going to get leveled, but it does mean there's going to be a bump from time to time, whether you're screening for the teammate with the ball or setting a screen away from the action.

So when you screen, make sure your feet are planted firmly and your hands are down. It's acceptable for beginning players to cross the arms across the chest to absorb a little bit of the blow. Bend your knees a little for balance or you'll get toppled over like a bowling pin.

Make good contact with your teammate's defender, and try to keep the contact for a full second. This "seals" the pick and stops any defensive momentum.

You must remain motionless—feet, arms, and body—when contact is made with the defensive player. The most frequent error is leaning into the defensive player, which referees quickly see and call a foul.

To roll, pivot off your back foot and use the hand that had been closer to your teammate as a target. Make sure you break in a straight line for the basket; that's the quickest way to get there.

Be looking for the ball immediately. Depending on how the defense reacts, the guard will choose the right time to deliver the ball. Make sure you never turn your back to the ball. If you did, you pivoted the wrong way.

Screening off the ball is a heady play that often pops teammates open. Again, it forces the defense to make an adjustment. And often the screener finds himself open because both defenders jumped to cover the cutter.

Blind screens, when the defender can't see you coming, are extremely effective, if you can handle the collisions. But make sure you know the rule: if the player being picked cannot see the picker with his normal line of vision, then he must be given one normal step before contact with the screen.

Screeners should keep their hands down and feet planted. Hold the contact for a full second.

76 HOW GUARDS CAN HELP

Dribblers should run their defenders into the screen.

The screener must be stationary. It's in the rules. So getting the pick and roll into the right spot on the floor is the dribbler's job.

As the dribbler, you have to run your defender into the pick. You and your picker should brush shoulders. That way, even the skinniest defender can't get through. A good way to practice is to run shoulder-to-shoulder off the pick and slap the picker on the back of the thigh as you go by. You are close enough if you can do that.

For screen and rolls, practice delivering the ball via both the bounce pass and the lob. You'll need one or the other, depending on how the defense reacts.

If both defenders drop off to guard the roller, you'll likely have an open shot. Practice making a quick, two-footed stop to get your balance and make sure you're not drifting left or right on your shot.

If there is no pick for you, the dribbler, you'll need to reward screens away from the ball by throwing good passes. Keep your head up: your teammates can set all the screens in the world, but if you're dribbling with your head down you won't see them.

The key is timing: players must wait for the screen to be set before making the cut to an open spot. And once they're open, it'll only be for a second or two.

Your team will score more often on screens away from the ball if the screener and the recipient are the only two players on their side of the floor. Adding a third player clogs up the passing lanes because the cutter not only has to worry about another defender, but his own teammate as well.

The guard should rub shoulders with the teammate setting the screen.

SIDELINES

9

77 HOW HIGH OF A HOOP?

To avoid fostering bad habits, put the basket within reach.

One blessing of those adjustable hoops gracing our driveways is that they make basketball accessible to everyone. It takes just seconds to lower the goal from the regulation of 10 feet to a dunkable level for even the most vertically challenged.

But how high should the basket be for a young player? It depends on the player, but here's my rule: no higher than one foot for each year of age. For example, an eight-year-old should be shooting at no higher than an 8-foot basket.

Remember, the most important thing for young players is having fun. Straining to get the ball up to the hoop takes away the most alluring facet of basketball: seeing one of your shots swish through the net.

Just as important, a too-high hoop fosters bad habits when a young shooter can't get the ball to the basket in a way that lines up his right foot, knee, elbow, and hand. He draws the ball down to the right hip, torques his body, then puts everything he has into his fling. His feet end up way left of the target (instead of directly in line with the basket) and the ball takes a crazy sideward spin, usually bouncing away in a miss.

The key to diagnosing straining shooters is the feet. If a player's feet consistently end up left of the basket, he's turning his body in search of power. Consider lowering the basket.

Besides, shooting a basketball involves eye contact with the front of the rim. Most players aren't ready for a regulation basket until the middle-school years.

Fortunately, many people are using the lower-basket recipe. Many cities are becoming involved in the national Biddy Basketball program, which requires the hoops to be 9 feet for the 12-and-under tournament and 8 1/2 feet for players 10 and under.

Organizers say that although most 12-year-olds are big enough to make a basket on a regulation hoop, the lower basket makes the outside shots easier and creates a game more like what the players would be part of in high school.

Remember to use an appropriately sized ball, too. Women's regulation balls are one inch smaller and two and a half ounces lighter than men's and are good for younger players. They're available at most sporting goods stores.

Young players aiming at a too-high goal often become discouraged and get in the habit of turning the body for more power.

78 CHOOSING AND MAINTAINING EQUIPMENT

Be nice to your ball and it will be there for you.

If you can't respect a perfectly round ball, play football.

That means when you're tired, sit in the bleachers, not on your ball. It makes it lopsided.

No matter how angry you get, kick something else. (Keep a soccer ball nearby if you must.)

Basketballs are meant to be bounced, shot, or held. Be kind to your property.

To get the most life out of your basketball, don't keep it in the trunk during the summer. Even if it's an outdoor ball, the heat causes expansion and causes the panels to crack.

When shopping, read the boxes and buy the ball marked for your use. If it says "indoor only," the jagged spots on your driveway will give you a crusty ball quickly. And those rubbery outdoor balls just don't feel right when playing on a wood floor.

Before you buy your ball, take it out of the box and give it a two-handed spin. Some balls are manufactured poorly and are lopsided even before the first dribble.

The boom in portable hoops means more decisions, too. Is it better to fill the base up with sand or with water? Who makes the best hoops?

Sand doesn't leak out as easily, so if you want a hoop to stay put, go that way. But if you have to move your hoop often (that's why it's portable!) water is more manageable. Check for leaks each time before you play: a top-heavy hoop can do a lot of damage to players or cars.

Before you buy a hoop, you may want to check with a local coach or athletic director. They likely have had some experience with such a purchase, and they are usually willing to help. At first it may seem intimidating to contact a stranger by telephone, but he'll likely be flattered, or at least consider it a necessary part of his profession. After all, what coach wouldn't want kids to be playing his sport as much as possible?

If you're tired, don't sit on the ball.

79 WHAT TO BRING IN YOUR GAME BAG

What all good scouts live by: be prepared.

The greatest predictor of who wins a war? The side that is most prepared. The winner of almost every major battle has been the side that showed up early. They were the more aggressive from the start, and the ones most "into it."

Most boys and girls can't always control what time they get to a game. Parents drive them, and there are often brothers and sisters with commitments that are just as important as a basketball game.

But the part you *can* control is making sure your stuff is in order. Most players carry a gym bag to the games; use that as your basketball briefcase. Here's a checklist:

- **Water bottle:** Don't count on the gym to have a nearby fountain. And sports drinks taste great, but they're actually more effective for the endurance athlete. Water is fine for participants who are on the floor for two hours or less.

- **Athletic tape:** Buy a roll at the drugstore. It's invaluable for ripped shoes or uniforms and for taping together jammed fingers. Trust the trainer if your team has one, but in recreational leagues trainers are rare.

- **Snack:** Sometimes games get delayed, and you might get hungry. Apples, bananas, and granola/cereal bars work well as snacks. Salty snacks can give you cottonmouth out on the court.

- **Change of shoes and socks:** If the weather is bad outside, bring your game shoes and socks in your bag. Playing with muddy shoes can cause you to slip.

- **Mouthpiece:** It takes a little practice breathing while wearing a mouthpiece. But going to the dentist to put teeth back in after colliding with an elbow takes time, too. Store it in a plastic bag to keep it away from the other items in your bag.

- **Scrunchee (if your hair is long):** Make sure what you tie your hair back with is made out of cloth, not hard plastic. The referees check, because the plastic could hurt another player.

- **Rule book:** Only if you like to argue a lot. They're 10 bucks at most bookstores.

- **Towel:** Dry off your hands on those simmering days. Sit on the towel on your way home to keep car seats clean.

Before you get out on the court, make sure your rings, watches, and necklaces are left in your bag (better yet, in your locker or at home). Those objects could hurt you or another player.

Your gym bag has items to help you do your job.

80 DRILLS WITHOUT A HOOP

It's not hopeless when you're hopeless.
Here's what you can do.

One wonderful facet of basketball is that it is the only team game you can play by yourself. You don't need someone to pitch or hike you a ball. You can get better on your own.

And you don't even need a hoop.

Here are seven ways to get better when you're stuck at Grandma's condominium with nothing but a ball and a patch of cement. Most of the drills involve a way of competing, either against time or against your previous best. Many of these drills encourage you to practice at game speed; practicing without some kind of pressure really doesn't make you better.

1. **Straight speed dribble:** Draw a line in your driveway about 30 feet away. See how quickly you can dribble down to the line and back. Make sure you dribble with both hands. If you lose the ball or double-dribble you are disqualified, because in a game either one is a turnover.

2. **Dribble around cones or chairs:** Set up an obstacle course, something that makes you use both hands and makes you maneuver through imaginary defenders. Time yourself for the course, and write down your best. Same rule on turnovers applies.

3. **Eyes-closed dribble:** Try to dribble 20 times in a row with your eyes closed. By dribbling with your eyes closed, you guarantee you are not looking at the ball. Once you get the hang of it, dribble like you are avoiding defenders, and try to cross over with your eyes closed. Make sure you keep the dribble below your waist.

4. **Typewriter dribble:** How many low, fast bounces can you do in a minute? Again, use each hand.

5. **Rebound practice (especially for younger players):** Toss the ball into the air with both hands. Practice catching it with both hands held above your head, jumping off both feet. If you are in your driveway, try to throw the ball at least as high as your garage.

6. **Imaginary shooting:** Lie on your back in your house and imitate your shot. Try to shoot the ball as close to the ceiling as possible without hitting it (keep Mom and Dad happy). Concentrate on getting your hand all the way through and letting your weak hand serve only as a guide. Be tough on yourself: grade each release as a miss or make. Think about keeping your elbow in and only your fingertips on the ball.

7. **Maravich drills (my favorite):** Pass the ball to yourself around your head, then around your body, then around each foot. Make sure you keep your head up, not looking at the ball. Then dribble around your body and around each foot. Then throw a two-hand bounce pass to yourself, in front of your body to behind. (See Tip 10, page 22, for a more detailed description of the Maravich drills.)

Set up some cones in your driveway and practice your crossover dribble.

81 LEARNING AGGRESSION

*Playing aggressively and competitively
applies to practice as well as games.*

Jump shots look pretty, but a few swishes don't often make a dent over the course of a game. It's more common to see the team that plays harder come out the winner.

While a lot of aggressiveness is inborn, a good amount of it can be learned. If you train yourself during practice to always play hard, your attitude will rub off during games.

Use the loose ball drill to get players in a feisty mood. Divide the players into two teams, and place one player from each team facing each other about 15 feet apart. Roll the ball between them. The player of the two who doesn't come up with the ball has to run a lap. Repeat until all players on both teams have had a chance. The team that comes up with the fewest loose balls after everyone has had a turn runs five laps.

The team part of this competition helps build spirit. After all, players don't like letting their teammates down—especially if there's punishment involved.

You can do a version of this at home with as few as three players. One player is the roller, and the other two vie for the ball. I don't think any unsupervised practice will involve lap running, but it's a fun game to play to, say, five points, and it provides a diversion from shooting, dribbling, and passing. Learn to step in front of your opponent, effectively blocking him out. The first step usually determines who'll get the ball.

Other teams work on aggression by having three players under the board battle for a rebound, with the rebounder trying to score on the other two. Once a player scores, they fight for the ball again as it passes through the net. The first player with three baskets is the winner, and the two losers have to run laps. For this competition to work, though, the players should be nearly the same size.

Think about grabbing the loose ball, not trying to dribble it. If there's a crowd around going for the loose ball, why tempt everyone again so quickly by putting it on the floor?

If you go to the floor for a loose ball, don't get up. If you do, it's traveling. You need to push the ball to a teammate who has hustled to your side, or call timeout (if you have any).

Girls who play pickup games with boys are often more aggressive than girls who play only girls. Boys offer tougher competition for girls not only because they have genetic advantages, but because the boys would hate to lose to them.

You can be well armed in the war of aggression.

82 HOW TO BE A GOOD SUBSTITUTE

A good attitude and studying the game are vital when you come off the bench.

Most basketball teams have as many players on the bench as they do on the floor. That means there's a good chance you won't start.

Attitude is the key. Your "friends" in the stands might call you a scrub, but take heart: they're not even on the team!

You can be a better sub than most by following a few suggestions:

• **Know the situation:** Watch the game intently. Know whether your team is in a zone or a man-to-man. Know what offenses your team is running.

• **Know whom you usually sub for:** If you likely go in at center, watch how your team's center is doing. Study the opposing center and see whether he has any tendencies. Is he right- or left-handed? Does he like to drive, or shoot jump shots?

• **Know when you'll likely sub:** A lot of coaches have patterns, or at least tendencies. Coaches often pull their best players in the final minute of the first quarter so they get a long rest because of the timeout between quarters.

• **Root for the players on the floor (at least outwardly):** Hey, part of you wants them to mess up so you can get in. (You're human, after all.) But being part of a winning team should take precedence over your personal wants. When you're out there playing, you'll have some teammates who'll reciprocate.

• **Keep your body warm and loose:** Stand and stretch at every opportunity, including timeouts. If you didn't play the first half, try to get up a sweat during the halftime break by hopping up and down and running full speed through layup drills.

- **Lower your expectations:** Most likely, you're not going into the game to be the star scorer. (If you were such a great scorer, you'd be starting!) So don't go in looking to fire up a three-pointer right away. Try to make a good pass or two, get the feel of the ball. A good goal is to get a rebound or loose ball every minute (or two minutes if it's a slower-paced game) and hold your man to zero points and zero offensive rebounds.

- **Hustle:** When you get in the game, many of the other team's starters may still be on the floor. They'll be tired, and you'll be fresh. Sprint for every loose ball you have a chance to get. Run as hard as you can getting back on defense, and fill the lanes on the fast break. You'll help your team, and—just as important for your sake—the coach will notice.

Above all, keep positive and believe in your team's system of play. If you make the most out of your few minutes on the floor, you're bound to get more.

Watch the game intently to learn the other team's tendencies.

83 BEING COACHABLE

A vital skill on the court: nod your head in understanding when a coach is talking to (or criticizing) you.

How does a good player become a great one? By listening to and learning from those who know the game. No one likes criticism, but everyone can learn from it. After all, feedback is the true breakfast of champions. You may not like it at the exact moment a coach is criticizing you in front of your friends, but sometime, maybe well after practice, think about what the coach said. You'll often find that there was some truth to it.

Coaches want to make sure that you heard what they've said, and there's a simple way to make them happy: nod. That simple gesture shows that you're listening and you've "got it," so the coach can go on to the next topic.

Your nod will increase your comprehension, too. Studies have shown that we listen with our eyes as well as our ears. By taking instruction visually and verbally, we are able to solidify what we learn. This has an obvious impact on basketball, where there is so much to learn.

If you want to save words and keep practices and games flowing, forget about providing excuses. "It slipped through my hands" and "I was fouled" are far from original, and it really doesn't matter. What does matter is getting ready to do it right the next time. Realize that sometimes you just need to play harder, and if things aren't going your way, reach for a mirror.

The good players are always learning. They constructively evaluate each performance, replaying the key parts of a game. Walk away with something positive from a negative performance.

The ultimate in turning a negative into a positive occurred in 1879, when Thomas Edison was trying to make the light bulb. After darkness for the 9,000th try, someone asked him why he put up with such failure.

"Failures? Nonsense," he said. "I'd say 9,000 successes. I now know 9,000 ways *not* to make a light bulb."

He eventually succeeded—because he looked at mistakes as learning experiences. Good players have quality practices. They know skills don't simply show up in competition. Game time is just a repetition of plays they've already made, sometimes hundreds of times before.

Players listen with their eyes as well as their ears.

84 RULES NUANCES

***Pay attention to the rules. Ask questions of a coach
or referee so you don't hurt your team.***

If you've only watched basketball games but not played, you are
familiar with the bulk of the rules. You know what a double-dribble
is, and you know if any part of an offensive player is in the lane for
three seconds, it's a turnover.

What's now necessary is to know every rule. That way you can
avoid the mistakes that make the difference between winning and
losing.

The only way to pick up all the rules nuances is case by case. Over
time you'll know the game well. Don't be afraid to ask referees or
coaches about rules; as adults involved with children, it's part of their
job to help you learn.

Here are some common situations that you may not know:

• **Inbounding the ball:** If you're inbounding the ball immediately after a successful basket or free throw, you are allowed to run
back and forth along the baseline to get better passing angles. But
any other time, like after the other team double-dribbles, you must
stay in a three-foot area, about the area for a normal throwing step.

• **Holding the ball:** You can't hold the ball for 5 seconds. You
also can't dribble staying put for 5 seconds if the defense is on you.
But if you want to kill 12 seconds, here's how: hold it for 4 seconds,
dribble for 4, then hold it for another 4. Just make sure you pass it
before 5 seconds are up.

• **Loose balls:** If you go to the floor for a loose ball, stay
down. Getting up is a travel. It's better to try to push the ball to a
teammate.

• **Block-charge:** The defense can be moving and still draw a charge. If a player on defense has what referees call *initial guarding position* (both feet and the torso facing the opponent), he is in legal position to draw a charge if the offense slams into him.

• **Kicked ball:** Kicks are called based on intent. A pass can hit your foot, but not be a kick. And another one that hits you on the knee could be, if you took a swipe at the ball as it was going by.

If you go to the floor to get a loose ball, push it toward a teammate. Getting up is a travel.

85 ATTACKING A ZONE

Good ball fakes will get your team the shot it wants.

A lot of youth teams play zone defenses to hide weaker players. As your basketball career progresses, all kinds of zone defenses will surface.

The thought process for playing against a zone is a little bit different than against a man-to-man. Most of the time the outside shot will be open—it's just a matter of the right person taking it. Driving to the basket is much harder because there usually are two or three defenders near the basket.

The key is to remain aggressive and to pick the right opportunities:

• **"Tighten" the front defenders:** If it's a 2-1-2 zone, for example, the point guard should try to dribble into the top of the key and draw the top two defenders before passing the ball to the wing. Pick one defender and dribble at his inside foot (the one closer to you). He'll have to take a step into the middle to block your path. This gives the player on the wing more room.

• **Ball fake:** Face it: playing defense is work. After awhile, even the most disciplined players will be lured by a pass fake and tempted to go for the steal.

• **Baiting defenders:** If a double-team approaches you, that means the defense has only three players left to guard your four. When the double-team comes, dump the ball off and let your teammates do the work. This helps players closer to the basket get open.

• **Think about triangles:** Before you receive the ball outside the lane, form a perfect triangle with your two nearest defenders. This maximizes pressure on the defense, because both defenders will be inclined to guard you when you receive the ball. That gives your team the four-on-three situation you're looking for.

- **Stay in shooting range:** When all five players on offense are in position to score, the defense has to honor all five. This makes guarding all of them much harder.

- **Remember to screen:** For some reason, man-to-man offenses often have screens, but zones don't. In zones, you'll know exactly where the defenders will be. When the ball is on the right side of the floor, try screening off one of the players on the left side. That leaves a teammate unguarded on the left side for an outside shot.

After players draw double-teams, there will be opportunities to score or draw fouls inside.

86 THE JUMP BALL

You get one chance in a game to do it right,
and the payoff might be a quick two points.

It's only one play in a regulation game, but it's worth doing right. Getting the tip—and getting a fast-break basket—gets your team off on the right foot. And if you score quickly and press, you're a steal away from getting the opponent to panic.

If your team has the person more likely to get the tap, you should take advantage of the situation. As you leave the bench after final pregame instructions, have a plan in mind. The tapper should have one or two players in mind that he will try to tap to. The team's best layup maker should position himself on the floor where he can streak to the basket with the least amount of attention. One player should stay back for defense and not let anybody behind him.

After both teams are situated, the jumper should make eye contact—just a little!—with the person he plans to tap the ball to. Everyone else on the team should be able to pick up the nonverbal signal.

Everyone should line up with both feet on the circle. Getting the ball is the number-one priority, and if you're off the circle the opposition can box you out.

You can gain about six inches on a tipoff just by logic. Here's how: The average jumper tries to tap the center of the ball as it comes down from the referee's toss. Instead, tap the bottom of the ball. You won't be able to tap it as hard, but with everyone standing on the circle the ball only has to go a couple of feet.

Another way to gain ground is to sneak directly under the ball as the official tosses it. That means your opponent has to reach over you from an angle, while your motion is directly vertical.

Sometimes you can steal a tap by making the opposition over-confident. That's why a team will use a short player who can jump high instead of a tall player who doesn't jump as well. It's just human nature for the person with the size advantage to let up.

The alternate-possession rule on held balls during the game has diminished the importance of the center jump, which is what the rulemakers wanted. But there's still nothing wrong with starting the game with a 2–0 lead.

If everyone lines up on the circle, you have to tip the ball only a few feet.

87 VOCABULARY

Basketball lingo: love it and use it,
or you'll be left way out of bounds.

By now, you know that good players communicate with their teammates. But as your game becomes more sophisticated, it's crucial to
make sure everyone knows what the words mean. Here are some
basketball terms that are a step beyond basic.

- **Clearout:** An offensive strategy in which the team makes
room for a player to go one-on-one. The rest of the offensive players get far enough away so their defenders can't run over to help.

- **Dead-ball situation:** A time when there is no action, such
as between free throws. The clock is always stopped during dead
balls, unless your league has special rules.

- **Floor balance:** Ensuring that four or five offensive players
aren't on the same half of the floor. Poor floor balance makes
defending easy.

- **Live-dribble situation:** When the player with the ball
hasn't dribbled yet. In a live-dribble situation, the defense has to
take into account that the player with the ball might drive.

- **Replace:** Usually the point guard is responsible for being the
first player back on defense. But when the point guard heads
toward the basket, someone else has to take that responsibility, or
replace him.

- **Reversing the ball:** Quickly passing the ball from the wing
to the point to the other wing. The idea is that the defense can't
run as quickly as your team passes.

- **Spacing:** Keeping teammates far enough apart so that the defense has to work hard to guard everybody. In many situations, it's 12 to 18 feet between players.

- **Stopping the ball:** What the first defender does in a three-on-two fast break. One defender will yell "I got the ball!" and block the dribbler's path to the basket to prevent him from going all the way for a layup.

- **Weak side:** The side of the floor that has two or fewer defenders. It's the best place for a halfcourt offense to attack, because it's where there is less defense.

In defending the fast break, one player's job is to stop the ball.

COACHING

88 ADVICE FOR COACHES

It's a coach's job to teach, nurture,
and make the sport fun.

Whether you teach them zone defenses or man-to-man, fast break or patterned offenses, your players will pick up that you're involved with something you like. And that can't help but rub off.

Everyone says you win with defense, and I agree. But every child loves the feeling of watching one of his shots go through the hoop. So the younger your team, the more time you spend practicing offense. The right way is to practice pieces of the game in drills, and to make every drill competitive. Then every time your players are on the floor, they have to do their best.

Layups? Give the team a minute to make 20. Three-man weave? Each group must cover the floor in five passes, can't drop a pass, and must make the layup at the end. (Otherwise, the players have to do it over.) Most teams practice the same fundamentals, but the teams that improve are the ones that practice them correctly.

Make practices active: moving is better for players than standing. If one player is dribbling to the end line and back while nine others wait their turn, they're wasting their time. It's better everyone has his own ball, and the first part of practice is almost like aerobics.

As far as offensive strategies go, I'd make my best player the point guard, regardless of size, and constantly encourage him to pass the ball to open teammates when they're in shooting position. Coaches too often place their players on the floor according to size, sticking themselves with undersized guards who just can't throw the ball far enough. Then the tallest players are asked to *post up* (which is way overrated) and catch the ball with their back to the basket and find a way to score. Not many high-school teams have a true post-up player, so what are the odds of finding one among a much less experienced group?

Defensively, it's between man-to-man (which develops players) and zone (which is effective if you have to hide weak players). Playing man-to-man gives each player a specific task, and gives coaches a reason to compliment everyone who steps on the floor, even those who never make a basket.

The number-one defensive tip to teach is to force your opponents to dribble with the weak hand. Teach your defenders to get the left foot forward, outside the dribbler's right hand. A majority of shots at the middle-school level come from the right side, from five feet and closer. If you can stop the other team from getting those easy shots, your odds of winning will increase.

The end of practice should be scrimmage time—it's the carrot at the end of the stick to dangle in front of players. I like to divide the players into teams and play a couple of games to three baskets, with the losers having to run laps or be last in line for water. (Again, keep it competitive: it creates a more gamelike situation.)

Finally, encourage the parents to back off, especially during games. (I've been lucky to have had excellent cooperation with this.) With homework, chores, and discipline, parents have plenty of topics for advising their children. Ask the parents to give their kids a break each day during sports, and let them hear another adult for a spell.

Coaches who love what they do will naturally develop a partnership with their players.

89 GAME CONDUCT AND DECORUM

Practice is over; it's down to business on game day.

It's game day, the reason for all the practicing.

The players reflect the demeanor of the coach. If you want a team that whines and points fingers, do the same from the bench. To a young child playing for the first time, you're Pat Riley, no matter how little or how much you know.

I try to get players to approach each game with a businesslike attitude. Spell out the expectations in the final practice before each game so they have time to think about what you said. Get the mind ready before the body.

The businesslike theme carries over into warmups. In youth leagues, the games are run off rapid-fire, so get the stretching done in the hallway before your team takes the court. Pregame is for as many players to get as many shots as possible and to get their heart rates going. If it's a layup drill, use two basketballs. If it's open shooting, have one ball for each pair of players: one shoots, the other rebounds, and they switch after two minutes.

Before the game starts, I have a basic rule of three teaching points, maximum. Any more borders on a lecture. On a typical game, it will be:

- "Let's do a great job on their number 32. Kyle will do a good job guarding him man-to-man, but everyone else be ready to help him."

- "If they open in a man-to-man, we'll run our motion offense. Justin, remember that the second cutter will often be open."

- "OK, team, we've had a great week. If we do everything like we've practiced, we'll be fine."

The keys are to be positive and specific. I've never found a general "C'mon, make that shot!" or a "You guys, box out!" to be productive. Instead, I'll say, "Drew, remember to put your rear end against his thighs" to get the box-out I want.

A good way to check your game decorum is to have a friend videotape your next game, cutting over to the bench at certain times. Then when you watch the game film, you also get a look at yourself. Sometimes we truly don't know how we act.

Keep instruction positive during timeouts.

90 CUT DAY

Honesty is the best policy, even if it hurts you—and the child.

High-school coaches make enemies each November. They don't want to; it's part of the job. The time they dread arrives long before the first tipoff: cut day.

We agonize over ruining a child's dream. I have watched some young people play basketball at summer camps since they were in third grade. Then I have to tell them they're not good enough even to sit on the bench.

Rejection of this sort usually does not help the psyche of boys and girls straddling puberty. It ends their careers. Not one cut in my seven years has gone on to make the varsity. And the tale about Michael Jordan being cut from his high-school team is inaccurate. In truth, he was told as a sophomore he wasn't ready for the varsity. That's a big difference.

The rejected players hang around for four years watching their friends continue their basketball lives. They sit high in the bleachers at games trying to blend in with their friends. They secretly (sometimes openly) root for my team to lose, to prove I made a mistake. At 14, they don't have the maturity to admit they couldn't handle the ball well enough, shoot well enough, or were just too slow or frail.

Some kids cut themselves. They talk during instruction time, they shoot when they're told to pass. They make faces during defensive drills and laugh off the fundamentals of a chest pass. Those are the easy cuts. They are also the exceptions.

Every year, when practice starts, I tell the prospects that we have room for only 12. Every year I keep 14 or 15. That's because there are usually 18 or 19 I want. And it kills me not to reward a player who has done everything asked of him, only to be vertically challenged.

My self-consolation: the line "It's the best thing for you" may ring hollow, but it's often true. One player who was cut had his winters free to become a state champion wrestler. Two more spent time working on ballhandling and shooting, and proudly showed me their junior varsity uniforms a year later.

I try to put the cut list up on Fridays. That gives the kids a weekend away from school and parents time to console them. But mainly, it gives me a weekend to hide.

Sometimes the players will ask why they were cut. Although it's uncomfortable to explain, I am honest because I have a respect for those kids. I think they will succeed later in life. Usually I'll cite their particular weaknesses and be as honest as possible. But occasionally there's a kid who just doesn't have it, and I'll resort to my ace: "Fundamentals."

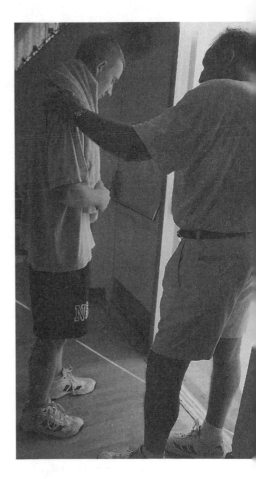

Cutting players is the hardest job coaches have.

91 MAKING ZEBRAS YOUR FRIENDS

Establish a good rapport with the referees. You don't need them as enemies.

Referees are people, too. Make them angry, and they're your enemies. Make them laugh, and they're your friends. So make them laugh. A jovial, outgoing rapport with the men (and women) who blow the whistles can only help you.

First of all, look at what it would do for you. Instead of stomping and whining, you're actually enjoying coaching. And remember, your demeanor rubs off on your players.

Your rapport should be based on future calls, not past ones. Saying "You missed the foul last time down" is no different than telling your player "You missed a shot last time down." Instead, you could say, "Please watch their big man; he's not staying set on his picks." In most cases, the referee will nod and say he'll watch for it. And that's all you can ask for.

Players should say very little, if anything, to an official. The fewer voices the ref hears other than yours, the more likely you will get the calls you ask for. And although coaches can't control the stands, one loud father with a booming voice can consciously and unconsciously sway the referee away from you.

Players do have to emote sometimes, so here's what I tell them to do. If one has a foul called on him when he thought he had a clean block, wait until he goes down to play offense. Once he's run that 60 feet or so, yell! Nobody will really know what the player is hollering about, and the referee doesn't get shown up.

The same goes for coaches. If you must beef about a call, at least wait until the next time the referee is within quiet talking distance. Any human feels alienated when dressed down in front of an audience.

And it has been documented that bad refereeing doesn't decide games. A study by mathematician L. Dean Oliver simulated 5,000 games between a good Team A (which scored on 54 percent of its possessions) and Team B (which scored 50 percent). In a perfectly called game, Team A won 70 percent of the time. Presuming the referees missed about 20 calls a game (a fair amount, though Bobby Knight would use a higher figure!), Team A still won 69 percent of the time, a decrease of only 1 percent.

Over five 20-game seasons, that's one loss. So spend your energy teaching better foul shooting late in the game. It'll get you more wins in the long run.

Talk to officials as humans, and you'll be treated humanely.

92 PARENT-COACH RELATIONSHIP

Parents and coaches should know their roles and expectations for each other, and treat each other with respect.

The older the player, the more responsibility he should have, and the less of a reason for parents and coaches to communicate. But basketball gives youth of all ages a chance to bond with another adult and gives them an example of how to handle victory and defeat.

It's part of the growing-up process for most children. If a ninth-grader has a typical problem with, say, playing time, he should discuss it with the coach away from Mom and Dad. It's part of training to be an adult, and it's a big part of the reason for sports.

Both parents and coaches should hold practice in high regard. Parents must understand that being part of a team means giving your all, and not only for the games—a lackadaisical attitude toward practice will rub off in games.

Coaches must treat practices as a time to teach, not to bellow. Good coaches want to walk away from each practice with at least one little facet improved.

Parents of younger players should discuss skills with the coach. Most of the time the parents have been involved in their children's development, and a fresh look from a coach could help continue the progress.

Coaches shouldn't tolerate parents verbally abusing their kids. If they observe a particularly critical parent, they should talk to the parent privately and ask him to tone it down. Many times the parents don't realize that they're being hypercritical. Conversely, parents shouldn't tolerate coaches who nag their kids into hating to play.

The parent-coach relationship flourishes when parents want to get involved and coaches want them to get involved. Coaches can involve parents with the following:

- Scorekeeping and timekeeping

- Snacks and refreshments

- Fundraising

- Setting up a phone chain to make contacting players easier

Involving parents with practice is trickier. For recreational teams, it's usually the more the merrier, and because the coaches are volunteers they appreciate the help. For school teams, it can cause problems and be unfair to the volunteer's child. No matter how good the child of the parent volunteer is, the player will be accused of getting perks because of the parental involvement. If the child is a bench player, what does it look like when that kid develops into a starter?

Parents who back off give children a chance to bond with another adult.

93 COACHING YOUR OWN KIDS

Make it quality time by following some simple guidelines.

With homework and chores, parents have plenty of things to yell at their children about. Basketball should not be one of them.

Coaching your own child can be quite frustrating. You want him to succeed, and you especially want him to avoid the mistakes you made.

Here are some of my thoughts about coaching your own child:

• When we adults were growing up, it was often just us kids at the games. We played for ourselves, and often there weren't even any bleachers. Maybe it's better to skip going to games now and then and let kids be kids. Talk with your child about it.

• The more you know, the worse it is. Keep any teachings basic. Dribbling, shooting, and passing are plenty for younger players. Leave the back screen for a reverse layup off the alley-oop for the pros.

• Think of it as playing with your child, not practicing. Rather than constant drills, invent shooting games and dribbling games you both can play.

• If you both are part of an organized team, get an assistant to coach your child. It will take some pressure off everyone.

• When your child succeeds, get out of the way. Give him his moments. (And if he doesn't have any, invent them.) We've all heard about how meddling tennis parents are; use them as an example of what not to be. Just think of how many young tennis players are out of their sport before they turn 20.

• Remember, you're there for your child. If you still love to compete yourself, play in an adult league.

• If the child wants a day off from basketball, take it. Basketball should never be confused with homework.

Make basketball fun, especially if the player is very young.

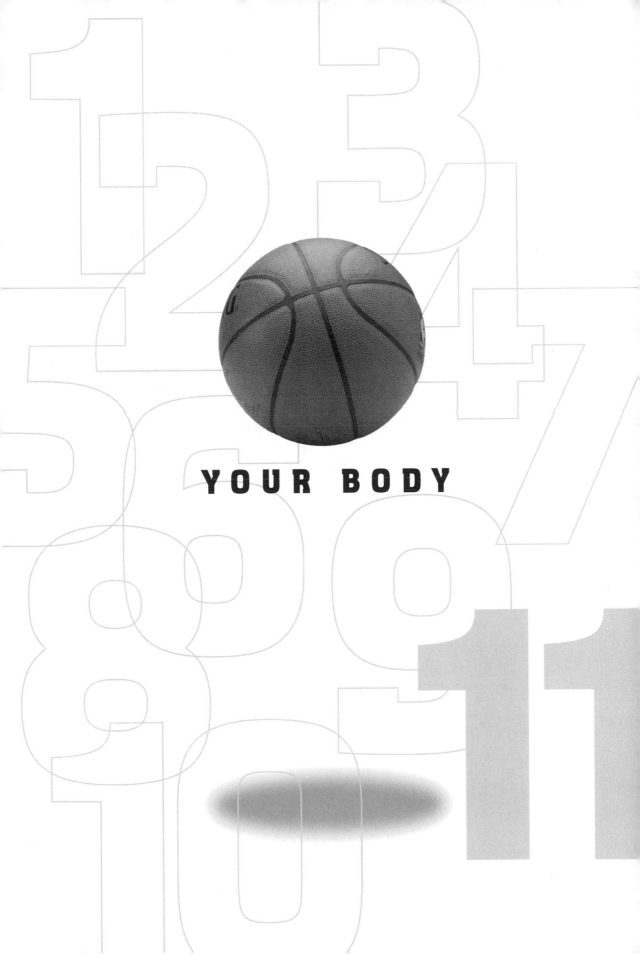

YOUR BODY

11

94 IT'S YOUR BODY

Get the most out of what you have. Conditioning, flexibility, and strength are key to physical superiority on the court.

It's the fourth quarter and there's a loose ball near your basket. You go for it, but an opponent about your size—who is just as determined as you—goes for it, too.

Who gets it?

The answer may have been decided a couple of months before the season. If you worked to get as strong as possible, and to be able to go as hard in the fourth quarter as you do in the first, then that ball may be yours.

The stronger and faster you are, the better you'll play. You can get better by taking care of your body. Conditioning, flexibility, and strength are the foundation.

Sure, nature plays a part in giving you certain physical abilities: some players are just faster and stronger. But you can make sure that you get the maximum out of whatever abilities you're given.

• Younger people should stick to exercises that are limited by their own body weight. Pushups, situps, and some isometric exercises help athletes build up strength without putting too much pressure on developing bones.

• Cross-train by using other sports. The two best are swimming and biking. Swimming builds up muscle and gets you in shape without any pounding on the body. Biking develops strong quadriceps and gives you a pleasant diversion from sweaty runs.

• Sleep is especially vital as a younger player's body is changing. (That's why teenagers' legendary sleeping habits are actually quite normal.) Just be careful on game days: it's better to get out of bed early, eat breakfast, and go for a walk than to sleep until noon. If you're still sluggish after the walk, then go back and take a nap.

• Look at your body as a jet, and the food you put in as the fuel. After a hard practice, high complex-carbohydrate meals (like pasta) help your body recover in time to play again the next day. And the difference between a banana and a candy bar for a midafternoon snack is huge: The banana is high in potassium, which helps your muscles expand and contract and prevents cramping. The candy bar will give you the quick sugar rush, but when the simple carbohydrate burns off, you'll feel sluggish.

But most of all, look at your body as something you'll have for a lifetime. Push yourself to be quicker and stronger, and over the long run it will happen.

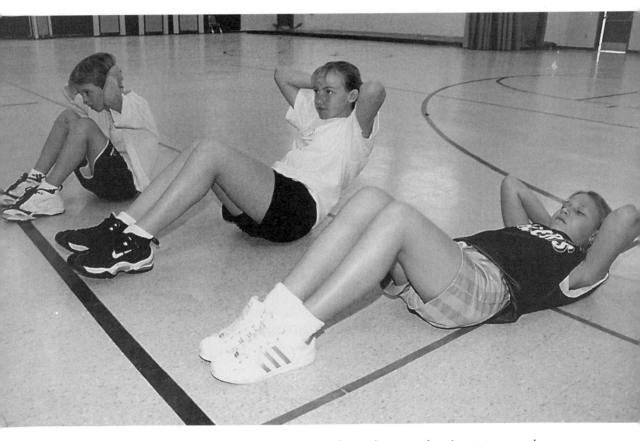

Situps and pushups are good for young players because there's not too much pressure on their developing bones.

95 RUNNING

Basketball means running for speed and for duration.

It's about heart. Your heart. Basketball requires bursts of speed, which fitness experts call *anaerobic activity.* But it also requires you to do it for a long time (*aerobic activity*). Your conditioning program should include both types of training.

For many young players, the first reaction to the words *conditioning program* is "Hey, I'm already in shape." But in many cases it's just not true. So you need to buy into the idea that to be the best basketball player possible, there will be some times that you need to push yourself beyond just playing in the playground.

Racing against the clock is the key. Set a goal for running, and you'll train harder than if you just trot around unfocused.

• **Aerobic conditioning:** If you have an organized coach, he will get you an aerobic workout during practice. That means the layup drill won't be just one dribbler and 11 others waiting their turn. Instead, 12 players will each have a ball. Before the season, you'll want to build what runners call an *aerobic base.* Runs of at least two miles (14 to 18 minutes) will help you with this. It's best to run with a friend, and if you can continue a normal conversation with just a little huffing and puffing, you're running at the right speed.

• **Anaerobic conditioning:** The only way to get in shape to sprint is to, well, sprint. During practices you'll have what coaches call *line drills* (they used to be called *suicides* until coaches began worrying about lawsuits). To break up the monotony, try dribbling through your line drills. It'll help your ballhandling.

Remember to run backward, too; it's a part of basketball, helps your hamstrings, and will give you a diversion in your training.

A favorite way to mix aerobic and anaerobic conditioning is at your local track. Three people alternate running a lap around the track (usually 400 meters), biking two laps, and resting. One person does each of the three activities, and everyone trades after two minutes. Bring a boom box and go through four to eight run-bike-rest rotations, and you'll have a good workout.

Conditioning and sprinting can come in handy in the fourth quarter.

96 LEARN FROM THE YOGIS

Borrow some stretches from the ancient Indian art form and feel calm all over.

Kareem Abdul-Jabbar credits yoga for extending his career at least five years. Phil Jackson offered yoga classes for his team in Chicago. If the NBA's all-time leading scorer and a coach with seven NBA championship rings see a benefit from yoga, that's plenty of testimony.

Yoga, an ancient Indian art, involves the mind and the body. That means when you're stretching you can't be talking about homework with the person next to you, or involving yourself halfheartedly.

Yoga is especially great for stretching hamstrings, and limber hamstrings are vital to injury-free basketball players. Taller people (most basketball players) tend to have back trouble, but often it's because the hamstrings are too tight and cause a pull from the lower back. Once that pulling starts, all kinds of things get out of whack, including the hips, shoulders, and neck.

The constant pounding from jumping also compresses the back muscles. Focused stretching (yoga) can help restore the space between the disks in the back and keep you limber.

Yoga stretching also teaches you when to reach a little farther. The body has more room to stretch on exhalation; so when you're reaching for your toes, go that extra millimeter as you push air out. Exhale slowly: think of inhaling for four counts and exhaling for eight.

Many of the stretches in the next section have yoga equivalents. In yoga, the back stretch is called the *plough*. And many of the backward bends coaches recommend are part of the Cobra series in yoga.

There has been a general boom in yoga nationwide, so there's a class for you even if you're not yet an adult. Teachers usually welcome anybody, and it's noncompetitive. You're working to improve yourself, not the person in front of or behind you.

Sometimes before games, you're going to be stuck waiting for the game before you to end. Then you'll have only 5 or 10 minutes to take the court. You could either sit around and moan about having to wait (the wrong thing to do) or quietly begin getting ready to play with some yoga postures. Don't make a big deal about it: just sneak away from the team a little bit, stretch, and breathe from your belly.

When your teammates ask why you're so calm, just smile.

Yoga poses provide relief for the lower back, which gets a pounding from basketball.

97 STRETCHES

Reach out and touch—your toes. You just might prevent yourself from getting hurt.

Maybe it's a rebound early in the game that you're an inch away from grabbing. Or it's a sprint back on defense to stop a two-on-one. Sometime during the game, your body will be glad you took five minutes before warmups and stretched properly.

The natural tendency of muscles not being used is to tighten up. Stretching helps you get your muscles at maximum length, and gives you a chance to get the most out of your body.

An added benefit is prevention of pulled muscles. And a hidden benefit is that if you do get injured, supple muscles heal more quickly.

It doesn't take much to stretch each time before you pick up the ball. Here are some good ones:

• **Arm circles:** A good way to get your body moving. Hold both arms out and make one-foot circles for about 30 seconds. Remember to go both forward and backward.

• **Standing quadriceps (front thigh) stretch:** With your left hand, pull your left leg up by the foot behind you, gently trying to work your foot toward your butt. Use a wall or a teammate to keep your balance. Hold for 10 seconds, then switch legs.

• **Hamstrings stretch:** In a seated position, extend one leg forward and tuck the other leg under. Slowly reach for the toes that are extended. If you can't, don't strain: just go a little bit farther with every exhalation.

• **Groin (butterfly) stretch:** In a seated position, lean slightly forward and gently draw your feet toward your groin area, with your soles together and knees pointed outward. Gently flap your knees like a butterfly; extremely limber players will be able to put their knees to the floor.

• **Back stretch:** Lie flat on the floor with your heels together. Then slowly bring your legs over your head. Go as far as you can until you feel a stretch in your back. Picture your toes touching the floor behind your head. Slowly come out of the inverted position, letting the vertebrae in your back release as your feet return to the floor.

Take your time stretching; don't strain.

98 WEIGHTLIFTING

Bulking up is OK if you have a little help from your friends.

Weightlifting is for the long term. A gradual, steady progression allows your body to recover properly, and you'll be less vulnerable to back injuries and pulled muscles.

As basketball has become more of a contact sport, there has been more emphasis on strength than in the past. Notice the body types the next time you watch an old NBA or college film: players who were once considered enforcers would be puny against the Karl Malones of today who bully their way in the paint.

Some guidelines for strength training:

- Do your serious weightlifting during the off-season. You don't want your body overtired during your season.

- Get good instruction. Find a coach or a personal trainer who can help evaluate your needs. Because each individual is different, each workout routine should be different.

- Use lighter weights for the first few days to avoid soreness.

- Make sure you're exhaling when you are lifting and inhaling when lowering the weight.

- When using barbells, always have a spotter nearby. (This also helps motivate you to do your best.)

- Keep a notebook with your progress, or put your monthly bests on your calendar on the 30th of each month. It will help you on those days when you feel unmotivated.

- Lift the amount that's right for you, not the weight everyone else is doing. True friends will respect that you are who you are; everyone else doesn't matter.

- Pick exercises that are specific to basketball. Bench presses develop strength for boxing out. Leg presses, extensions, and calf curls help speed and jumping.

- Work on your wrist strength. It will help your passing, shooting, and dribbling.

A lot of high-school teams have weightlifting programs during the off-season. They succeed because the players push each other—and feel indebted to each other.

If you're new to a school, even if you're not a star player, being part of the weight-training program is a good way to break in. There's time to bond with your teammates before the season starts—and everyone can use more friends—and you'll earn their respect because they see you're willing to put in time away from the cheering crowd.

When you're ready to begin weightlifting, worry more about form than the amount of weight.

99 CONCUSSIONS AND OTHER INJURIES

Be educated on common basketball hurts so you'll know what to do if something happens to you or a teammate.

Players should know how to treat their own minor injuries and know what adults will do when there is a major one.

The good news about basketball injuries is that most of them are minor. As the game has become more physical and aggressive, it's not unusual for players to get nicked up. Many school teams are providing sports trainers, qualified individuals who advise players on even the most minor of injuries. If your team has such a trainer, consider yourself lucky: most of them care deeply about both sports and children.

If it's a recreational league, players, coaches, and parents will often be on their own. The universal advice for minor injuries: you can't go wrong with ice. If a player jams a finger or turns an ankle, a plastic grocery store bag and a handful of ice will provide immediate relief. If the pain persists, go to a doctor.

Basketball injuries are usually one of two types: head injuries (concussions) or soft tissue injuries, ranging from contusions to fractures.

Here's the vocabulary many trainers use:

• **Concussions:** There are three grades of concussions, which is a shaking or jarring of the brain. Grade 1 is the more prevalent "bell rung" type, where the player never loses consciousness, but may be confused momentarily. It's usually OK for players to return to the game 10 or 15 minutes after the player returns to normal.

For Grade 2 (short loss of consciousness, like after a player's head hits the floor) or Grade 3 (2 to 5 minutes of unconsciousness), it's best to call 911. Players should be inactive for one to four weeks after such incidents, depending on the severity.

• **Soft tissue injuries:** These include bruises (treat with ice), dislocations, fractures, strains, and sprains. There are three degrees of strains and sprains. First-degree is with mild swelling and some pain; second-degree includes muscle weakness; third-degree occurs with complete instability and loss of range of motion.

For the most part, trust your body. If you try to play and find yourself limping or holding an injured area, you're not ready to return. Wait until you can enjoy playing without having to think about holding back.

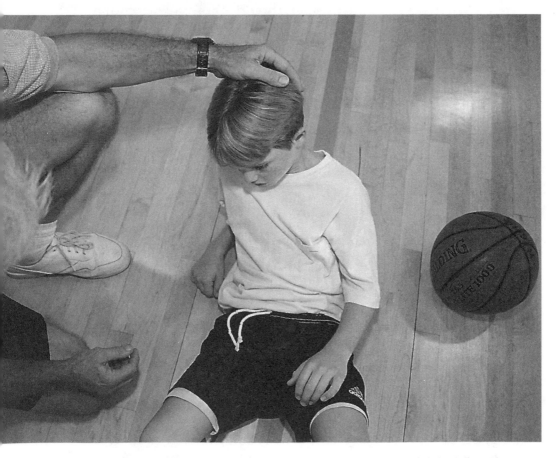

If there's no trainer, a coach or some other adult should see if a fallen player is woozy.

100 FIRST AID

Being a step ahead can help you during unpleasant times.

Players injured in games will get plenty of attention. There's either a helpful parent, an extra coach, or (if you're lucky) a trainer on hand to help. But at least two-thirds of all basketball injuries come during practice, when it's just the players and coach, or during unsupervised practices with players at parks.

Here's what players and coaches should know to make that time easier:

• If you play a regular game at a gym or a local park, know beforehand what you would do if a serious injury happened. Who would you call? Where's the nearest hospital?

• Keep a few bandages and a roll of athletic tape in your game bag. If you have any special medical conditions (such as diabetes or asthma), have documentation of that in your bag. If you play on a school team, make sure the trainer knows ahead of time if you have any special medical conditions.

• The first few minutes of an injury are usually the most painful. Remind yourself that it's going to get better very soon. A sprained ankle or dislocated finger can be excruciating at first, but within 15 minutes becomes manageable.

• Reach for the ice. There's nothing better. If you're icing your ankle near a basketball court, though, keep it wrapped in a towel and elevate it if you can. Water dripping onto the court can quickly bring you some company on the injured list.

• Remember basic first aid. Cleanse any open cuts or wounds. Apply direct pressure to stop bleeding by holding a clean cloth over the open area. If you are unable to stop the bleeding with direct pressure, seek medical assistance immediately.

• Even if your friend swears he "can pop it right back into place," don't let amateurs handle dislocations. First of all, there might be a break that could be aggravated. Second, you should leave your body to the professionals.

• Treat overheating injuries for what they are: a life-threatening condition. A player who has dry, hot skin but is no longer sweating, or is dizzy or having chills, should be cooled as quickly as possible. Douse the player with cold water quickly, get him to gulp down cool liquids (unless the player is unconscious), and get help.

• If you're a coach, consider taking a CPR class. Most communities offer them.

Finally, always keep learning. Know how to take care of yourself so you can continue playing this wonderful game when your hair is gray—or gone.

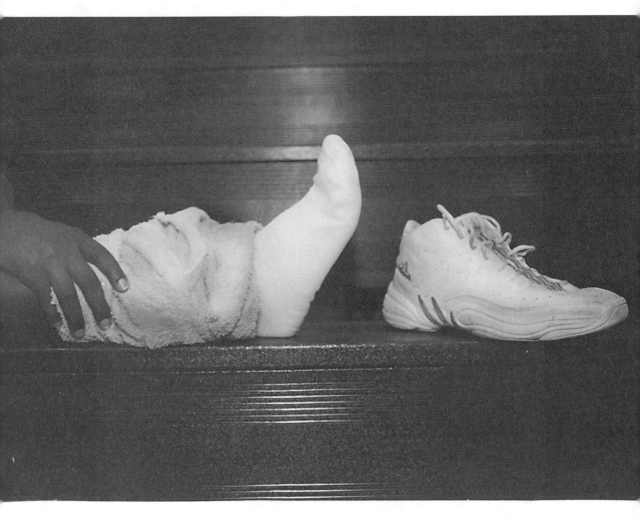

You can't go wrong putting ice on an injury. Use a towel to prevent water from leaking onto the court and endangering other players.